Mid Life

Also by Michael Haslam

various ragged fringes
The Fair Set in The Green
Son Son of Mother
Continual Song
Sothfastness
Four Poems
A Whole Bauble
The Music Laid Her Songs in Language
A Sinner Saved by Grace

MICHAEL HASLAM

Mid Life

Poetry 1980-2000

Shearsman Books
Exeter

Published in the United Kingdom in 2007 by
Shearsman Books Ltd
58 Velwell Road
Exeter EX4 4LD

www.shearsman.com

ISBN-13 978-1-905700-39-4

Acknowledgements

I would maintain the acknowledgement made in 'Continual Song' to J. H. Prynne and to Tim Longville (it was Tim who asked after my 'punctuation policy'. And I realised that I hadn't got one). And then I acknowledge the editors of *Poetical Histories, Equipage, Parataxis, Angel Exhaust, Active in Airtime, Conductors of Chaos*, and *PN Review*; and especially to Michael Schmidt and Carcanet Press, for bravely midwifing the monster *A Whole Bauble*.

And further, to Tony Ward and Arc Publications for enabling the Song to continue beyond.

The publisher gratefully acknowledges financial assistance for its 2005-2007 publishing programme from Arts Council England.

Contents

Mid Life: In Preface

Attempting coherence by hindsight, the plot of my writing seems clear enough, as a three-part venture. First, what I might call various ragged poetries (1963-1979) which I don't seek to suppress or censor, but which I can neither commend nor make cohere. The contradiction here was between inspiring Modernist ideas, of spontaneity ("first words, best words"), the "break with the pentameter", and the free placing of words in the space of the page, and, in contrast, a practice which, from early on was using re-writing, over-writing, transformation, on an iambic pulse. In this context, eccentric word-placings (I came to think) were merely making precious something that was as run-of-the-mill as flowing water.

Around the time the Conservatives and the Monetarists were beginning to reshape political Britain, I began to try to pull myself together. *Mid Life* might be a period between, say, 1979 and 1999, or, in publication terms between *Continual Song* (1986) and *A Whole Bauble* (1995).

Composing 'Continual Song' was a matter of gathering, rewriting, transforming all that I'd written to date, that might have been located nowhere, in language, in myth, or out on the coasts of tourist vacation. What I wanted to do was, bring as much as possible into the place I lived, the Upper Calder Valley. The conceit that the book might be read back-to-front was based on the fact that the front parts were the most over-written, the back parts the newest, and more spontaneous. I thought that reading back to front might constitute a journey from freshness into the Rewriting Revelations. I'm not sure, now, that this works. And though I do remember the mechanical procedures, I can't, but for rare instances, detect what the rewriting might have been rewritten from. When all I was rewriting was 'Continual Song', the book came to feel complete.

The Open Township marriage years (1985-90) were the hardest. Trying to be a publisher, and a Creative Writing teacher, didn't aid writing, but the hardest thing was that, as the marriage deteriorated, the wife took to seeking out, and finding slurs against herself, in any scribble I might be engaged in, and these became the foci for furious rows. I'd plead innocence and abstraction, but since I'd theoretically accept responsibility for anything that might be read into my words, my case was weak. The result was that my scribble became something secret, hidden even from myself. When the end was in sight, I gathered this scribble together, and published 'Aleethia', a sad farewell to poetry, and the last act of Open Township.

The trouble with this sad conclusion was that it proved not to be true. Free open scribbling resumed. The next work, which has had several titles, but is here called *Something's Recrudescence through to its Effulgence* began with 'three simultaneous poems'. I attempted to write the same poem in three quite different versions, out of unhappiness, in hope that I might cheer up somewhat. That hope was requited. In fact, I went over the top into the joyful daftness, the over-effulgence of 'A Fourth'. Meanwhile I was able to rewrite 'Aleethia' (as 'The New Aleethia') to remove the untruth that it had been a dead end.

It will be clear from this that the plots of sexual relationships have been a prime source for the generation of poetic plot, but also clear that the poet has not proved a satisfactory husband or lover, on the whole. I attribute to my Lancashire background the ambition for the Poet to be, above all, a Comedian. For a stock comic character, the Laughable Lover is pure gift, and it's part of the humour that the foolish boyfriend cannot always see the joke. 'A Fourth' came in time to give me problems, to seem to be merely bad and silly poetry. The three (I felt) needed a fourth, but the fourth was unconscionably foolish. I produced mangled and awkward revisions of it for The (sound) Archive of the Now (2005)[1], and for my website (2006)[2]. It was only this month (November 2006) that I came to believe that the poem knew what it was doing, and knew that it was only me who had been the fool all along; that it's a successful satire, but that I, in my person, am its butt. What had led me to reject it was a joke that I was failing to laugh at. The love affair that 'A Fourth' celebrates came to collapse in the bizarre and farcical parody of a drama of the 1970s, touched on, in previous form, in *Continual Song*, and involving a variation on some of the same characters: The Lady takes up with The Poet's male friend. You have to laugh.

Though I was quickly embarrassed by 'A Fourth', I was still in a mode of effulgent composition when the invitation came from

Carcanet to produce a *Collected*. In no mood to objectively edit old work, I resolved to rewrite almost everything (CS excepted). I excluded much of the various ragged poetries, but included some re-writings of pre-*Continual Song* things. Some of these were so rewritten that their origins were unrecognisable, and they became new poems, though placed to the front of the book. Other pieces (of a developing Image Phantasmagoria) were placed towards the back. I had an idea of the grand Bauble structure I was building. It's unlikely that a reader would grasp what I was at.

Here, as by default, the order of inclusions follows that of *A Whole Bauble*. It could be otherwise. Excluded are a couple of sets I called 'Vacations', in which I'd, rather hurriedly, against deadline, tried to rewrite various ragged fringes and some other stuff. I made a mess that I can only consign to the recycle bin of ragged poetries.

After *The Bauble* I worked upon a long poem of humourless agony. I've managed to forget its title. My ruling Comedian judged, rightly, that it must be suppressed, buried, lost.

The current project, which I call *Music*, with Arc Publications[3], began at the turn of the millennium when, over fifty, I realised that I wasn't young, and that, if I am to live long enough, I should prepare for the poetry of old age. It therefore lies beyond the scope of *Mid Life*.

Notes

[1] www.archiveofthenow.com / Here can be heard the 'three simultaneous poems' of *Three of My Chasms*, and an odd late attempt at A Fourth.

[2] www.continualesong.com/ Here the reader may find notes to references and allusions, and information, possibly 'too much information', on biographical background to the poetry of *Mid Life*.

[3] www.arcpublications.co.uk

A Century
Continual Song
(84)
&
Aleethia
(16)

Continual Song
(1986)

'In one of the Icelandic sagas we have a strange story of a man standing at his house-door, and seeing the souls go by in the air, and among the souls was his own. He told the tale, and died.'
  – S. Baring-Gould, *Curious Myths of the Middle-Ages.*

'Tri Dyfal Gyfangen oedh gynt in amser y Brytanniet: Bangwr, a Chaer Gariadawg, ag Ynys Widrin. yn Sasonaec Continuale Songe . . .'
  – Rachel Bromwich (ed.), *Trioedd Ynys Prydein.*

'I like to describe this in Ovidian terms, as a carmen perpetuum, a continuous song in which the fragmented subject matter is only apparently disconnected. Ovid's words are:
  to tell of bodies
  transformed
  into new shapes
  you gods, whose power
  worked all transformations,
  help the poet's breathing,
  lead my continuous song
  from the beginning to the present world.'
– Robin Blaser, *The Fire.*

'Some of these songs . . . cannot be sung.'
  – Charles Ives, *Postface to 114 Songs.*

WINGS
      in a blank white shining room
blind me so I blanch and finch
and blink still at the white
of walls and floor.

    Wings of The Idea
      of the Advance of Being
Human, sprouting from a Sphere.

 A zephyr rushing
   to the visible from the invisible
and filling lungs.

A falcon falling out upon the wind –
the vocal remnant of illumination so sustained
until it disappears inaudibly.
   Here, take these token wings,
an interruption to an argument,
a stop upon an outrage and an anger;
may they carry you through areas
of Spiritual Danger –

   the infernal haunt that hurts internally,
and funnily enough I must be blanked with wings
of wishing prayer, 'May the Planet
be washed also with these wheeling winds.'

02
83

My growth in all its senses springs
of sharing in the sex of an inheritance;
an intercourse whose being is
in shouts and silence.

   At the entrance to the spring
         there is an atmosphere
   of streaming rising wings;
a Figure pointing forward through election
         to the threat of war;
a shining wind across a reservoir;

freaking airs about the court
   of a transparent palace.

I place my dumb cross in the deaf booth;
exhale waste which empties in the shrill,
      cold in the ears. A silver wind
makes for a silver wake. I hear

how hollow freedom sounds through broken flats –
the agents boarding up with nails
      the broken windows. See
the soul slip on her steps of stone.
A hunted look spread fast across her face.
      The sound of helpers yelping after
helpless madness fighting off remote control.
      Stop there upon the stair-well! I can hear
her shouting echo through a hollow hole.

Orient Pearl. The rising glow electing glaze
    of blue, and colouring accumulates, tinting
spectacles of light. Wild rose growth springs
    out from the arch over the waterfall.

An apparition on the bridge, a stranger
in the pure white clouding of the sun, a figure
in all innocence sways in his silence, when
the limping Spirit of Impatience, keen
to close the daylight gate of dawn, pronounces:
    'Now the day has come, your daze is done!'

    A ringing gong. The light is decorate
        with azure and gold strings.

Clouds curdle, clown and tumble over down
and silken green, crowding the bridge to blur
the blue-er pasture.

    Key-ring dangling from impatient fingers.
        One more look, I'll follow on
    the homing drone through crazy static –
        let's not talk, but look there
           outlined like an angel
            is the sparrowhawk
            over the brook.
        'OK. Let's walk!'
    into clear tone,

a small town in the early Sunday morning.

Aquila in the rainbow. *Angel* strangely
indicating an oblivion. The way
    the car stopped at the crossing, with the coffin
running through the doors. The coughing stopped.
The ghost came to the window where
the terrace steps were overgrown.

The hoofbeat of a deer in wild Old Caledonia.
A tolling off a tidal islet – Belling shapes
of spectral light across the sand. *Aquila*
at the key-points of a life's romantic thriller.
Secret agent caught communicating notes between
the car horn and The Golden One. The crucial
    Figure, of a Shepherd or a Gardener
who keeps his flock of flowers. Park-keeper who
minds the cemetery by the ring road, while the
blue blasts of exhausts perfume the air.

    These keys. A film of scenes. A burst of beer
and laughter from The Seaman's Hall. Street-fighting
glazes as I pass through quiet breaks. The fighting
on the steps recurs. And there's
    Alanna, Angel, or *Alauna!* as I call her –
Passing by she shakes her hair and nothing more.
    Was I to greet her or to warn her? but her
laughter left me sitting on the jetty after, waiting
for the island bell to tell my time again.

Flapping, on the wake's cold frontier, who we were –
Souls in Adventure, children bound to colours
of allegiance, in their own religious thriller
pleading at a barrier to be let pass.
   'The wine is red!' – *'Aye, red as blood!'*
Like cliché snecks or latches into dream.

For a beginner, there were agents through
      the false door shouting, *'Who*
are you working for?'
      I seek the peace, a prince who settled like a bird
upon a beach. A bleached white page –
blue shadow of my fingers, curling a pen
      along a line. Bright sand. A sound of beauty,
but they make that noise to drown us out.
Either it thunders
or they bang their pans in din.

I concentrate my mind and hands to scrape into
      wet sand. My nails strike slate. I enter shimmer
of some summer. Mummy calling, *'Come on in for dinner!'*
I fear the world is wheeling backwards to a shallow
      moral shadow. Leaden sky, a flash,
an autograph, the shadow of detention.

The historical romance is in ascension, when
the flute goes up a scale again, dissenting
trooper trailing voices cross the moor and march
disconsolately on into the atmosphere, and vanish
absolutely on a whistle. *'Run along!'*

On the Avenue to the Aurora, Fortune may turn glamour blue and sunny in succession. I confide in echo: I have horse's ears. I thrive on fear. I want unconfidence to thrill me senseless faith. I drift to the Romantic Shores and camp upon the pagan version of transliteration: baffled in a haze by all the doors I face in trepidation, shaking in my pants.

Doing building work I learned to fake: to point and render blank; to make a show of coping like a proper man, and flash exceptionally with the genius of common sense. But one bad job, a bodge, cemented in a muddle, wakens infantile incompetence. I come to consciousness of the pretence I'd solved the riddle in my drift, and left a clean and clear defence of moral vagrancy, exhibiting a state of sheer complexity and deep transparence; I had sealed the roof in a perplexity of rhyme, a work made proof against the weathering of Time.

Natural initiation presupposes soul or substance, something like bituminous solution I neglected to apply. Suppose I die upon the avenue to the aurora, having no more faith than I was born with in responding to a human face? Deep subject with his echo cooing; cloud and uncloud, smile or cry; in or out of love. Feeling disgrace and pride and hope to goodness, *Goodness Knows,* not knowing what the heck I think I'm doing –
Fortune turns to Mark whose Glamour chooses.

Matching, sorting out, the neuromantic sense of
secret order haunting what is heard as harmonies
in music, folklore, and romance. Restarting from
the minute brightness at the centre of a startled
moment: almost at once appears the figure too much
misted on the sorrow headland, when the private rush
invading falls far short on the wet bland ebb,
the dome-encoded globe is being broken
on the estuary sand.

                    Far out
            Shearwater as *the earth is* spinning
an embodiment of spiritual intelligence:
She emanates a beautiful green ray.
She radiates a deep blue sea
Imperium of Legend,
                scattered light, a vibrancy
                    cloud shadow
                        light blue sound.

Against a day of waiting for a train
that almost never came; a force defeated
and a door flap flapping open over ocean
out of sullen leaden cloud.
        I try to shut it out. I match and cling to bits
of brightness, a transparency in wind,
a key blue sound,
the vessel visible and coming conscious,
            blessing,
                shimmering in space.

To perfect tone would be its healing;
crossing the moor into a storm,
Let hail obliviate *my feeling!* Cross
to whom this would be sign
of weakness. I'm eliminating lines,
more lines than I care to remember;
but how long, how long, my journey is!
to be delivered from the millwheels'
faults and truths and squeaks.
    Out over Lancaster the sky appears heraldic –
    Plumes of argent on an azure ground.
    I come to the pass and see white light;
    rain bullets on bent grass and rushes
    surfaces all fresh and clean.

Images that used to speak in squeaks
of unoiled wheels now stop
and let me be revealed –
    Who is this wounded soldier
bleeding from his private parts? who is
this piglet squealing from the womb?
Who am I, shivering like one
saved from the cold sea, making song
and dance of his natal inadequacy?

Upon this pass I cross and let
go all of that
below the pitch of soul appealing,
dropping to a trough of the amorphous wind.

Within the air of being guarded by the Crows, I
query:
    'Is she sky, the Shekinah?' I'm shaking in the
spectre of a bliss. A flash of sheen off
feathers. Crow Twins guarding the Aetheric
Boundary.

    The crows as like as swallows are to bring
the weft in threads on wings, and crows
hard beat down wind in the Advance of
Storm.
        As like as swallows to appear, the cross
in silhouette with gulls against the sunset,
or to show in beauty that it's all a veil.
        Over the library steps, the factory gates,
the traffic-lights, the leafy avenues, the
brick and aluminium chimneys,
        pylons, motorways, and skies –

    The ring of clog-iron on cobble.
Guard it well. Avoid. A wail
off siren for the shift over the street.

All such impediments are lifted off.
Today the ordinary bands are being broken.
Air is swirled and bristles warning.
Fingers of inversion mist evaporate in blue
blue air, and butterfly articulations flap
and flit into and out of it, till Crows
arise to show the wings of blacker void.

10
75

Whist,
        fall silent, hear the roar
within the ear,
the intermittent bleating of the sheep,
the pleading of the heart before
        The Golden Bar
in the Silent Court
of the Daylight Star,

a footstep on the gravel, deft, too near
the heart, a horn, and *be on guard!*
a shout, a car door slam,
    a lavatory rinsing. Windows
blankly glinting, chisel ringing
on the new estate, wheelbarrow squealing,
    empty endlessness and worse.

Whist else a whisper; she's
the outcome of the airs who
in her disappearance glances twice.
    A whistle, and the sunlit blinking lid
sounds down the steps into the deafened heart.
She draws the blind. Her train of rushing green
blows blue-ish as it enters under ground.

      The brink of pure abyss remains
        no longer dangerous
      but out of bounds, and passing
        key blue sounds.

The Swallow dives into the wood
as if for the last time.
All the colours of the earth are dying.
Moths flit over gossamer and purple heather;
flocks of small bright birds alight on
tongues of fern jutting abruptly from
a tumbled limestone rubble dry-wall.
     On the final glimmer an affection flashes
off the hill, over the spires and clumps of trees,
catches a glass and lights the fairy tree
of feelings. Streetlights burst to bloom
the moment stars appear to net exchange
across the day to day.

Or from the flash of dawn there follows on no sound,
no thunder and no metaphor or form.
The moment stars or night or daylight fade
the sun or moon strikes down upon
the tin roof of the Standard Tyre And Exhaust Centre,
or moonwind on the wave.
     The gauges change while moments star
and sparkle in the air. My fear is that I have
no place on earth,

and unspeakable flashes zig-zag through the sky.
The Dark Wood Aboriginal.
It is the thinning of the veil to take a dive,
a dip into the depth of time alchemical,
as rich as colour dye,
just to be written in inconsequential weather.

Rainbow light.
    A spatter beds down dust.
The sandstone slices cleanly on the grain
like slate. It rains. I break
for tea and sandwiches. A cigarette.

My living forms my need to write.
I hurt myself too much. I smoke
and breathe cement and silica dust.
I lose my touch. I know I can abandon work
and walk along the moorland brink
imagining my life is real and I am
who I am: it makes me grin to think
I have arrived at some predicted station
in the course and depth and space
of private life. The view becomes a land-mark
    and includes my boot-prints in the peat
and Stoodley Pike. I look back to the farm-house
where I have abandoned work. My tools lie there.
The world has sure solidities and all is well
and so I touch the wall.

I need my small recuperations filled
with providential chances brought to hand
by drift as secret news of one
subjective rosicrucian sort of
world of truth. The living forms
I live my life in *rainbow light*
and dwell in illustration.

Rumpling felled me: I felt helpless.
Drift lifted and dropped me off,
stopped on the hapless spot.
A dead line closed;
    the railway-line closed down –
the gas-lights broken
    and the paving overgrown.
My only suit of clothes, inside my bag,
    was crumpled hopelessly.

Shadow figures in the depth of tunnel vision –
drug-crazed anarchists exploding bombs
to wake the fuddled and corrupted Giant State
and send recriminations roaring through The Underground.

    It only takes a single cell of six
    to set the system echoing with outrage
    at the Wicked Servant standing in the bright
    hallucination of his own malodorous alarm.

    I saw one once in his black overcoat
    vacating a train.
    His face looked haunted at a distance;
    playing games with The Omnipotence
    infernally,
    some hope to be made whole.

14

71

What wet cold clouds crowd on
about the house!
It stands up under buffeting.
I keep my upstairs warm.
I waste my breath on bedroom windows,
hear
rejoicing of the wells for miles around –
Astounding Waters!
Marvellous House in the clouds!

I'm being domed in domicile.
What sound is being made?
What clatters in the clough like that?
The axe bit in the wood with cliff of stone
and water echoing below, how sound is
delicate and elemental.

I'm being made a Keeper as an image,
grail or house or ground. I'm game
and laugh, brushing the stairs, the broom-head
and the bristles touching woodwork. Lucky

to care for the spider
and to tend the fire.
14 Foster Clough
'71

Eyes opening upon a piercing lawn of dewshine.
Palpitations dining on a pan of blood.
The whole white shield of the protection overthrown.
An angel bleeding on the ground.
 Sleepwalker walking on an August shore.
 A creature calling at him: *'Did you not know
 the doom has not been found?'* or, *'What wit-
 ness is there to our fucking doings?'* Shouting
far too loud. Who'll flail you for your frailty?
Who can tell your failure from your blatancy of tone?
 Ravenous preacher prating from the pulpit
of a broken heart, whose seed falls like your
flour of snow on stony ears.

I saw the gypsy in full summer moonlight once upon
the shining road, casting a glamour
as a gossamer on gorse;
 a figure blasted by a van whose fuming
diesel funnels sound and leaves a ditch of silence
and a mute surround.

From my terrace I can see through tears
a rising starting from the heart of spring's
ignition, and a winged sphere whose
beauty and whose purity the earth confutes
with stars, and I'm out of my body completely –
see the light collecting in the leaf,
the old back-yard, the old back-streets –
I can unbar the gate and see the mill
machinery disgorging sheets.

Seal dreamer, Demon woman, Dragon lover,
   Phantom mother;
Roll on Ye Waves onto The Desert Shore!
What if there were no Throne?
I'm still enthralled –
Deaf as the flocking sea.
White fleet, half-light, half shade.
   The grey seal screens the swimming scenery –
a louder sound of bells along the coast
     Proclaiming Rain.

We sailed that coast by stars and found
blue mountains to the East at dawn.
All morning long we sailed, and watered
where a brook debouched, and reckoned
ourselves lost.

Car Mirror. Flash Light. Horn down into Foggy
Hollow. Broken Code. The house cut off. A seacoast
morse. A bleating ghost. Waves of alarm leave
marks. Small bits of glass defeat the heart.
   The accident is inexplicable. Still breathing
soul. Still lies. With beating heart and lips
apart. Low tide. The seabirds plucking lives
   off terribly desolate shoals.

Bells louder from a tidal islet. Jetsam
at this point. Remorse. *Return!*
before the storm. The ghost remains.

The door slam. My,
how the years are passing! Returning
The Hidden Church of The Holy Grail to the house
with dark oak-panelling, and pictures in the hall.
    The door slam. That's the wind-sign
of October in a more occulted Zodiac.

    Crossing a bridge to a conjugal bed, we stood
to hear a long dreary commotion off the ocean.
Lapping Alleys. Breathing Sighs. Long Shore.
    White Wood. The moonlight
on our hands and faces. Roar
continuing after the clap-trap shut. Not lost
for what to do we strove to put a soul
into the void, clothed with the Royalty, Originality,
Virginity and Genitality of intimate size
and private capacity –
an infinite appetite to drown.

    And parted like the term of freedom.
Cold wind with the tidal flood across the bridge
in greenish light. Old Woman in a shawl
holding the parapet, a flapping signal
of the world. Opacity. Opacity Invisible.

I think there is a secret order hidden
in the passage of the world. A stifled cry
trapped in a dark room cupboard years apart.
    A path of lace curls up the wooded scarp.
    An owl hoots out of the dwarf void.

Sneeze! in the stuffy hayloft –
     Swallow fluttering wall to wall–
A blue glint in the lightshaft
flashed out through the door.

The brief life which the Druid thought just flitted
through the hall, fleshed out with feathers. She is
     emblematic mistress of the lucid transmigrations,
dumb speech to the wise. *Hello!* to my
life's brief bedfellow. She's
the blindfold soul pursued by dogs
of the inhuman world –
An object of remote control, who touches home
     The Sanctuary Rock, with fingers crossed
Over the water,
as the options close.

She stays to make a web of ways
into an inner chamber. Threads
     the days of my amazement
          through an open door, and sways
to weave the pattern of the sacramental moment.

Hear her Praise!
She's us!
The Sister Radiance!
The spectral daughter.

19
66

The bone signs screaming through the sky-screen.
Hysterical scenes of conjugal debacle
in the house cut-off by sleep and dreams.
   The day breaks on a plate. *Over.*
   The crackle ceases on a hiss. *Over.*
A streamer is the road before my feet.
A spoken sound. A broken horn. I voice
      the dreamer in the house left dangling over
         dereliction cliff.
The dawn is time to go. My coast is clear.
   The ghost of mind adrift.

A rose light globes of florid sleep
to cover loomings of the shadow lover, spun
to weft the woman cut off in the house of death.

A wailing blueness speaks out of the East
along the street a coat of light yet lemon pale
and not another soul apparently about,
   only a flight of geese, report of horns to greet
me at the quiet gate. The traffic-lights
alternate, motionless, the morning waits
upon a milk-float: bottles in their crates
   start an uncanny rattle. Bones. The ghost –

not quite hysteria, and short of fright and sleep
I hesitate and settle sight. Take in
the outcry of last night, and let the float
go down the street. She curdles to a cream across
the wake that marks, *Awake!* my parting walk.

Bright rubbery alert about a
suburb roundabout. A car departs in
sonic burps, diminishing to saxophonic
bird-like flight. Such bursts of a superb
cacophony! I leap about a bit and jump
and sprint in brand-new tennis-pumps.
I tried to thumb the beeping thing.
    It leaves a trail, a blue-ing wake,
a wailing echo tail, lying the length
of dumb blank bedroom windows.
    I whistle blues, absorbed in streetlit
leafage. Joy to be a poet and a part, compounding
synaesthesias that time can't decompose.
    Eruption in vibration empties as a bubble
glows. To be in love! – and moving fast, to be
escaping trouble on nocturnal highways, the
blue-purple of the past.

    Alighting in a drift of smoke, a missed
connection. Party voices calling through a party
wall. Electric beat *zap! zap!* of Pinball City Music,
    a succession of blue light-bulb rooms, and
each blue room a stab of pain. I blew a fuse
    and saw the spread of Time in dereliction,
valueless, and footloose among strangers, singing
to myself, mischief, and far from home! –
    Alone, and pitched abruptly
into metaphysics, pathos, and curdled corruption,
Never To Return!

21

64

I'll give you this:
            it rains,
the quietest thursday morning
            in the story of the world.

There is a magpie in the mist. Apart from this
the only traffic is the vans of largely
nationalized concerns. The only growth
I can detect is in the dandelions and grasses
        in between the flags. What else
            is intermittent as a barking dog,
a skriking jay,
a solitary crow's voice over the far
fog-muffled ever-present hum of morning cars
moving along, and then a goods-train
seals the green-belt in a mortal absence.
            Take this girdle.
And a cow in pain pierces the sluice
as though a suicide,
as earthly as unearthly.

All this morning soul is lawn
evaporating off the hill.
A cat comes patting quietly
as daylight on the flags.
            I raise my arms to shoo some sparrows
out of mischief. Something almost wakes
for half a moment at this false alarm.
        It is the day that sleeps
            which has no needs at all.

Austere desolation at the border stone.
A loss of faith.
        And all I saw those years was but
the scuffling of some kites and crows,
daylight and dark,
the shifting of the vault of stars,
the sunlit water surfaces,
my bootprints in the peat.
        I was attending wells upon a semi-desert
fringe. I wished myself away over the mosses to the
coastal saltflats, over coalfield silent window flashes,
cotton-mills and crosses, washing drying in the wind.

The sky was fanning and electrical –
A flapping crashing sound so beautifully . . .
then drowned out.

        The tray of teas, winged death,
the new estate, the silent space,
the wrought-iron squealing gate, the rush of steel
around the cemetery ringroad.

Beyond the gypsy outskirts of a Northern City,
a deserted house, the plaster scored with
sexual graffitti.
And by night the streetlights make a jewelled snake
out of the villages.

All wrought as one
with rotting windowframes and falling rain.

The haunting crescent blare of trains:
A Time-Warning: Beware! –
Too suddenly our twining strains.
      The nomad with his hunting horn
      is no more out of key nor blurred
      and fabric-torn than we were
      dumbly running with the herd.
Screwing against the grain this turn
the valley sounds metallic.
Fell display of yelping hounds for quarry
from the school-yard in the breaks between the bells.

Inhuman Spirit of The Hunter! You
who lead me through the Winter!
      Lapwings hanker spectro-sexually, flap
against the blanks in cross black clouds
between bouts of blustery rain.

The Calendar turns inside out.
The Year is sprouting birds about.
All daylight is the aspect of a starry atmosphere,
      with washing flapping in a drying wind.
Dismayed and Undismayed by turns.
      Wet dismal drapery.
The hollow scoffing like a drain
      until the changing quells us
to the estuary, bearing our remains.

24
61

Transparent airs curl tendril forms
        of fever and delirium.
I heard
that Ellen May,
that Ellen may have been reborn
clothed lightly
as the fragile dweller
        of a spacious dawn.

I stepped out of my shadow-darkened home
to see the cotton-grass on the horizon,
distant sunlit farmhouses
and valley shadow folds.
        A goodstrain in the distance seals
        the old blank pain, the well
        whose shell remains.

We are together
standing in the doorway
of the sleeping dead.
She holds the sewing threads.

She shakes the breadcrumbs from her apron
for the birds, up at the ruin, over
on the other side – but when?
A Century Ago. They call her
        bleeping, shrilling –
all her nature's morse.

25
60

I broke my breath on baffled vast
expanses of Atlantic Vitrine
Aquamarine Serpentine
Sea-green and azure silver

Deep blue sea
a foreign policy
a colour code in colonies
entranced in Time Immoral
History of people singing fighting
drunk on sea and wine

Purple Imperial the past
A Crow wheeling to grass
punctures a corpse a ghost
the aura of a host to clothe the vacancy
A Christian his last
coastal romance death and rebirth

The sound of people singing on promontories
The birds
The brittle rash of arms
The laughter of the earth
I broke my breath
it smashed to bits
a globe of glass on granite

a return
by gravity to earth

The death of the brain imagined ending
an extreme of pain. A shout
at the door. Slamming the storm out.
    Making sound
space inside stone or concrete blocks –
    a sure defence. In definition,
an *enceinture,* ringed and safe
which opens inward on

    a fulmar plashing on the night sea pasture,
sheep flocking in waves under the window,
    white bird on the curling breakers
plucking lives off surf.
Moonlit, entranced, in winsome bliss.
    Keeping Warm

No sound.
What's this? *ah hiss* –
    it passes breath.
What was that horse of speech an angel rode?
Dumbfounded now dismember
    on the path to the estate:
Initiate, come to the wrought-iron gate.

    Step over!
Piping on the pass.
ah hiss.
    What was that noise?
The plumbing of an angel in the storm.

Beyond the terminal post-war estate
  with broken windows
    useless phonebox corners
      a Continual Waste
        wind over broken pasture
        Vents
      through broken walls and gates and intakes
ruins and vacates the shell
blanking fluorescence, battering
a shelter for the sheep
out of the weather.

    White wind on the reservoir.
    An inborn human obstinacy cheers.
    (Make up a hearty being here:)
This is the Land of Empress Helen of The Wells.
    A crown of elderflowers glows –
    roots riving out the walls –
a heap of stones with nettles overgrown.

    Wind encompasses its self-consumption
    in vacuity and leaves all else
    in sway rotating
    Water on the wind. All Else
    as Ellen. As Continual
    as Weather Wind and Wells.
(Call it 'Brigantia', or else 'Tall Tales'.)

28
57

Ah anima, be broken on the granite coast.
    Mare, la mer, yr hen anghofus fôr,
Illuminate in light, breaks in a shiver,
    dissolution, still englobed.

The waterfall throws up a spectre of its spray
against the blue diurnal veil.
    It's aureate, or, everything's ok.
The bell of animation babbles
    beautifully golden well.
Bubbles globe from globe to globe ensouled
in an astonishment irradiate with Spirit –
Words pass out of sound and use and sight.

The sea-horizon today is hazy and the
greenery a special light –
Fair fountain of eternal juice.
The blue is silver in the winds of truth.

The Ancient Self is broken into tongues upon
the crust of the Asian Shelf. Latin and Welsh.
A coat of feathers. Rumours. Tidings of
a Spiritual Being wholly permeate. Romance
    of *anima, l'amour, arrival.* Being broken,
globing in the light of hollowness
    of space in colour, spectra
        of a healing happiness.

Slow rolling bands of shadow channel
undulation echo in the bass chamber –
a cavern in the brain, a haven
in the headland where reminders
are retained. The rushing and relaxing strain
of waves in passing left a mark
of froth, and that *forever,* kiss, embrace
the wave and cross the stain, the stone,
with insulation of *accept forever* loss.

The mere flash of a mirror in the aftermath.
A hand that waves or wipes the steam off glass.
'*Walk on!*' the wave had seemed to say,
and I walk on my own, in my own boots, on my own
feet, my own light head on my own shoulders.

A foam-white noise of wells enveloping
a white horse at the ford. My boot-thump puts up
doves from bushes. Gulls light from a ledge
and shadows skim across a beach of boulders.

Sea and River Waters. Waters of The Wave. What Are
Your Voices, Eh? Oracular the rolling of *Yr Afon* –
what with flits of foam, the thumps of stone,
my doves and moths and other bits
of unassimilable disappearing shade.

How deep the emerald of moss is. Mark
and emblem lest it fade, and *Yes,*
Remember, Cross.

The chisel slid, I hit my little knuckle
on the chamfer edge, and bright red globes
of blood accumulate, and with the clouding
they coagulate, and six doves swoosh
  to seal the suffering, the pain, the sore,
the harmony of vanished worlds on fire.

Each Word The Dead shout through
The Trumpet of The Ear has been distorted.
Through an utter wizardry the sun is turning blue.
It was a dreamer going into code
  in coded gloom. Lunatic
Window-Wall Proportions. Dead Loud Shouting
  Echoes in the Shape of Things,
along the avenue, the prospect of a
clouding of an ear.

The pain bout clamours more inaudibly.
Some people die of a broken heart.
The day she drove the van away it seemed
the fabric of the land had ripped
and I was standing in her slipstream bare
but for my tatters in the wind.
  Look after thyself, then.
Loud Shouting Echoes in the Shape of Things.
Small clouds of sweat evaporating swiftly
vanish in the heat.
I am the keeper of my body and my love.
I seek a cigarette, a break,
  a left-hand glove.

Clear light, an air of glass
through which light celebrates itself.
Clear shadow of the hawkweed on the meadow.
Dockflower clear and slender as a flame of rust.
An orange scarlet pimpernel.
Clear sound of gorse-pods popping.

When the sun sets (over Sennen) birds are
silhouetted, and my shadow blends into the dark.
I see peculiarity
       in my original as death,
unclear,
and undistinguished and at home in darkness.

Clarity of light escapes my art
of writing. Writing of the clarity
escapes a breakdown.
I can hear a wagon changing gear
as starlight saturates my poor . . .
              (unclear—
poor dear, poor heart, poor home,
poor hearth, poor eyesight or poor ear?)

Pour on, ye Agents of The Pure!
As rhymes occur, the brain begins to blur.
Return to her!
The starlight rains down on the fields
       and on the shore.
I wish it to effect a cure.

One day's feeling is of light
    and the wind the light illuminates
across the grasses.

The Sun is this day's shepherd
    as the wind comes to a whistle
driving a flock of cumulus to sky-pasture.

Sun, who flashes over water: Ecstasy
Of No Extinction, beckoning or beaconing
on deep green glass
    close to the source.
Just one Green Spring is all it takes
to fill the bowl
of a becoming whole.

Who is this shepherd metaphor?
I float upon the reservoir
and face the light,
feeling the wind lick like a dog
across the surfaces.
    I don't know if it's Christ or it's
Cernnunos, or the simply deep
atomic sun and wind. I simply feel
it fill this spacious waste.

The crux is this. It's His,
My Deep Green Shepherd.

I *saw a man clothed with rags,*
his tatters streaming in the wind,
reading his fate in fear that shakes him —
talons of heart-sick disease that seize
upon his neck and shoulder muscles.

  Under the shadow of a sullen
  Luciferic spire,
  Great Land-birds wheeling round about
  Above a dull laborious mire.

Can he not see the steps he has to take?
The semaphoring of his Good Evangel flapping flags?
I see instead his sense of life careening
through the pasture, the impatient traffic
horning at him, children laughing, women
wailing at him, all the ring-road
screaming, and the whipped sky cream.

  His own Salvation
  his appointed dream,

wherein, the space of which is vanishing,
the traffic has to be held off
for him to see his way to cross,
    the weight and burden
    to be lifted, lifted off.
Salvation has to be a scene for this
to be believed, if seeing is believing.

Across the floor a glass is smashed.
A thread of sticky something numbs
insensible a thumping in the ear.

I suffer flight into the violent
Romance Exaggerations
flashed off an axe up in the air
with cups and glasses smashed across the floor.

The Crow comes for me with his Wings
Enveloping.
She stands beside him wanting blood
from me or something
       Thumping
    Thumping.

      Are they playing darts
          or making baby infants
        in the loft up there?

They take my eyes and take my innards,
fly out
    slaked and flapping
through the open door.

35
50

That dumb spot I can't obliterate,
    I go back over
water breaking on the sound of voice

        where one white van moved off in time
        its unburnt fuel exhausted.
        Crows and lapwings rise
        from a field of grass.

I try to keep the vocal chamber clear
but phlegm re-flocks into it.
Waves break on the sand
of vast desertion.

        This I swear is where I saw her
riding with the host of them.
The brake burnt through, the lining gone,
the shining ones go through the wall
into a field of cries and lapwings rising

        where the stop is terminal
            a dumb
        confounded spot

seeing the broken glass, a smash,
the witness blotted –
black specks rising from the blind spring.

Greyness widens with the dark receding
and at four a.m. she came from him
to be with me for May Day Dawn,

and we climbed the rise and saw the sun
squeak briefly sandwiched in a bed of cloud
so much the mouse and nothing of The Dragon
or the half-apparent Pagan Man revealed.

We saw only our failure and our
future that went unfulfilled, and there
we were prepared to leave it, when
The Angel Life came travelling
a shade too fast, and flapping,
had to bank too steeply at the site
of vision
and he crashed between us.

Since that bloody intermission
        now I can't recall
            The Angel Bleeding
or observe the dawn
        without
my pulse rate speeding to record
    uncertainty of ground.

Clusters of ungainly men appear to clash
across her face. I'm going to have to
give her up. I'm going to have to give up this
mysterious ground for good. I'm down to rounds
of blank blank blank.

It was the end of May when in the flight
of the retreat I found the garden
Actuality in tears, and really flowers
and a wellspring and a helping hand –
a miracle I felt I'd been provided for,

until the rival forces came to spoil for me
this last resource.

I'm going to have to give it up –
no longer give ornate or decorated shrift
to genital affection.

Garden bleared with verdure
where the cock got fucking shot
I'm giving up
the bloody Orient,
the bleeding Pearl, the bloody World.

I used to think of Pan and Christ as
kind of twins
    and heed the bleating heart, the
shepherding of shadows, thundering
and mushrooming and dancing rings

and sought for omens as enlightenings –
    the wagtail on a stepping-stone,
a heron on the river-channel on its own,
and through the trees I heard some wings –
a thrumming and a trailing drone, some anagram
or palindrome, some sort of lonesome soul
a-tamping on the ear-drum
    who could you do you
        bird in plume you jenny
    wren in bluebell spinny.

I used to think as twins under the aegis
and the star of Venus,
    but the one whose Love is Charity to us
had grown severe in his impatience
with me. Gone again
and I was madly
sprouting horns and gladly swearing on
    my thumping heart.
My face is like a faun's, my hairy fetlocks ...
    See how my trail is grown! I fart
and let out of my mouth and soul
the old complaint, the sounding wounded breeding call.

The light falls softly through
the stained-glass taproom window
of *The Weavers Arms*, through pipe-smoke,
into pints and onto playing-cards.

The light falls graciously
The Queen of Hearts
I love you
Angel a Leo
Little Town of Todmorden

I want to let *I love you* emblem and
include us both alike without alarm
at least until tomorrow morning
and to let go more

in lines of shivered fitfulness than I have ever
dared or done before, until our being in the light is
more and more restored.

Funny how lovelily
a little healing hurts.
Funny how lonely now my
feeling lives by fits and starts.

Cold shrill loud March, lapwings and larks
across the slack make quick the coital
breeding clocks, the crystal year
whose pulse is jugular, whose pulse is silver.

Beside the hearth there's talk of springs
and chimes and balances of antique
time-pieces, and talk of honey-guides
to draw the bee into the throat of this
Narcissus. Please

let's have no more of persecution
in the glassy echo-chamber
stimulus-response. I'd rather just
enjoy the curtains of embroidery
and draw the border portals on our
golden age, the olden gate, against
the grating days of scraping wrought
iron mars the pitch
of bloom onto plate glass and screeches
of amorphous satire. Let's

kick back the sheets
and let out longer lines as valuable
as semen spasm or as argent whispering.

Labouring with scutch and wire-brush, at Little Manor,
Heptonstall. A crash of plaster-dust reveals a date over
the door: *1681* –
    that rings a bell with a Miscellany of marvellous
things – all London bells ring in the delph, the den, the
concave quarry of the ear, and in it echoing I heard:
    The Lord, The Lord is my – Waterfall.

Re-hammering time after time along a line, I reckoned
with the issuing of Reason from The Nation, taking care
not to and yet, *damn it!* my hand slipped and I chipped a
little sliver off the date. The thing's defaced. I break for
cigarette, and flask and sandwiches, and take a step back
from the whole unconscious opaque wall into the world
of Will, the likes of Angels, and the Genius of Mankind,
and take a piss and think the issue used to matter to the
meanest Private and assembled Corporations of the
living land – whole companies – a singing led them on to
an Ideal Invisible.

How few remember now the inner Commonwealth
    of *Gonganora!* How that Conscience
in his bloody Courage slashed across the core –
    A Century – the corpse too good to have been
fought for. When primeval Silence finds us
    thingless, standing in the loss of aura
        of a Crown,
            My Heart heard *Gonganora!* ringing
                Town to Town.

The Angel Life

Like crows, a wheeling company blows over flags
and broken windows, leaving in its wake
a Corporal who, plucked in tumult from the fray,
demobilized, has wings closed over him
and he is saved.

The broken habit of visible light shows up in dumb
handwriting on the page of cards. Come back from wars
he trails his wounded imagery to the angelic surgery.
  I think it is my aura that is hurt. Good Lord!
Shining a flashlight on, *My Goodness! It's my heart
I see surrendering in there!*
  And, being willing to surrender, all the wayside
changes. Rhododendron flowers on the glass canal
reflect a slow beat vacillation. Pace the heart.
Lift left, the gift, and right, the grace
of vacant space.

  A touching takes me. Is my singing
still so dissonantly shrill?
  The worst is past. Well, bless my soul!
A silver knowledge! *You did well.*

Funny how focal though the funnelling became,
to have to bear more honestly the writhing in the ear,
all hours, colours, callers, bells and flowers,
funeral horns and halls and blows, the flow,
the blaring waving and the healing calling –
Once Upon A Time Life Tenant.

No Bloody Matter

The slightest vacuum when the concrete-mixer stops
before the birds return the song of wild exactness
as a cartridge to the chamber
        opens a gracious jewel atmosphere of space:
Amazing Reservoir! The miles and miles
of water pouring through
            to no point in retrieval.

Water consciousness is sound, and listening
I'm weird in thought and scents of peace
between the breaks.

                Each day I'm thought
                by themes of hurt
                and beat my fists in air and take
                Tobacco,

until signs are made to dowse me through
an avenue into a perfect chamber.

Here as a slave I wash my sloths out
in a water music enclave, while
all sorts of sorry doors and courtyards
safe from breezes
ring with antique charm.
        And quiet in the centre of a circle
in the square appears
a whole side of the body-image
weeping or disintegrating,
bleeding like a fire at the extremes.

For these drowned in the tumult of the civil fray,
the way-crosses remain, a nectarine
to sweeten body-pain, the hyacinthine grove,
a bluebell spinny, and a wooden glade.
    Good Lord, what felonies were done,
    that doing lately gone, now funny,
    lonely and alarmless, listening
    to waters lap

    I guess I've been too much a snatcher
after the aetheric wrappings, catching
senseless cold and napping threads invisible
now that the looms have gone
and there can be no restoration now not ever.

Funny though how local clues
who call you from the delph
across the clough – It had that
sudden echo shadow
    Cuckoo!
in which lines were drawn
with skirmishings that came to nothing.
    Cuckoo calling come and gone
    but seminal, a flurry in the scenery.
    Cuckoo!
The drowning men still smiling,
dining as so many butterflies
on flowers of the field.
Aubade and Nocturne.

The mocking gurgle in the foibled ear:
O Gonganora! Gonganora!
The invisible commonwealth is here
Encaverned, crystal clear

with blue light on the pool
and primrose flora of the year

to grace the bower of our intercourse
in conscious innocence and water light
on both sides of a glass and light
and shade chamber – a camera to take
the always personal, always interpreted
fluorescent pulse, penumbral and ballistic –
falling sleepward in a shower, falling slower
into coital lock and even lower,
my enamoured, to the base, a cavern
hollowed out of shock.

My, I do admire you Heart
You are so wonderful, You
Keep on beating, and I
Hear you rush with pleasure
In the light of praise.

And here I speculate into the dwelling
of divinity in human mind and heart
as well as in Pythagorean Area,
bi dum bi dum bi dum bi dum bi dum.

Ogres. Orgasm.
    I feel shaky for my organ star tonight.
October Moon
    throws a switch to throes of ice
and darkness
    and a Crystal Turning Throne.
Doors of The Night,
    the sway of wind in alleys. Has me reach
for something starry, watery, and glamorously bright
    exploding in a glass –
Or else it's cryptic silences, studding the records
of abandoned drift, a dead morse code
gone cold as a white torch.

Organs. Orders.
    Breed on Impulse. Teachers
numb me with my dumb mistakes. I blame
the fire powers, the higher face of fear,
the shadow, and the flame across the floorboards.
    Vagina. Copulate. Originate. I cross my parts
and rush to tap a glass of water, make
a bee-line for the telephone and call My Flower,
bubbling on the surface with the need to mate.
    The Queen of Ogres sits upon her Throne
and has an Operative in this world take
the call. *My Love.* Need we manipulate? I'm wrong
to call you, her most sweet capricious minion.

47
38

The public space turns sharp as glass.
Life suicides itself. Undress.
The living in this place so poor that death . . .
I cough, the clock ticks perilously close
to failing. Coldness cracks my lips. A frost
covers the glass.

    The face of death appears in blueness.
I see eyes in a midst of ice,
polar extremities without survivors. Cold dry wind.

The space abstracts to show the axis turning.
Planet Earth is *recognized* from stellar distance –
Blue-White Crystal Turning. Spinning rings
around its self-eclipse, elliptical
in Periods of Force.

    Electrical, the brain recourse
to warm itself with zaps of sensitizing song,
continuous in pitch, impulsive swinging, electronic
song affirms the brain to be the seat of silly wit
at an extreme. It says that this is not My Death,
    Curl up and warm thy belly!

Scanning rhymes enhances chuckle-rings
advancing from the heart and lungs
and makes me laugh out with the sense
of warm blood and elastic innards.

Glow in the Sky. Tremors of Fear.
Day doesn't die, although I know one day
will clothe the doorways of the ear with daze-
    embroidered curtains
        on the brink of dawn
and all but all my attributes be wreathed
and ringed and floral,
    entering a Giant Yawn of Space,
the sleep-invader of a Gaunt Oblivion
for all Humanity. A mass of suffering
arises in a mist,
    a still green meadow, since the stress
and in the silence of an aftermath,
the blue forget-me-nots, a stream, a woodland path,
a garden, a memorial, a Chapel of Rest –

    Or Else, Midnight is Real.
    I am in Hell, and don't
    want to be Recognized.

Old woman on the bridge at dawn.
A snaky light on the Thames, orienting pink
and yellow, rose and grey, before the plenitude
and heat and light of day, when Sun will beat
like bleeding Heart, *bomb bomb* on heaps of scrap
and motor wreckage.

    Iron Walls,
    The City Has Iron Walls.

Father, Mother, hear me, this
is the hour of my naivety,
Nativity?
Where does it come from, *Mother?*

Smothered in the feathers, figures
Fingers? stand like icons, *Acorns?*
birds and bees pass in and out our
hollow spaces
and the sparkling bells of sound.

    At a late hour, the gate is shut
and the Keeper, who is one among the many
images he keeps, on this island and others,
Jangles his Keys

Lord of The Trees, Oak Shadow, Harbour me
Among the Wharfs and Warehouses of Dis,
Upon the Battlements of Troy, Do Not Destroy
The Stone of Earth and all its colour tones –
Jupiter, Saturn, Mars . . .

What, That Motley? Their time is done!
Their end is come!
Their doings sound all wrong.

    A swoop of crows collapse out of the wind
to feed upon their acorns.

Venus, source and sorceress of trouble,
riding in the sky, shines in a lake
of light revealed in low black flying cloud –
    Observed and Unobserved, Unominous
and Ominous in turns –
    Turns eyes upon the figure skating
on the surface of her influence
among eternal Obstacles,
the golden structures of a mobile Universe –
A chiming rink, a charming ring.

I see a bright mind moving on ahead of me,
drawing my clumsy feet and fingers after me.
I see a Spirit fretting
over Mental Institutions.

Now the skating figure leans its body to
    the bright side of the Year
and sees *so deep, deep*
    deep, so deep,
sighed in the ear –
    the code is blurred.

Venus, a hawk-like woman
peering through the sky-window encourages
The Skater with his courting skills
    onto her Birth Canal.

Today I drowned a dying cat
quite quickly in a lukewarm tub
of water. As I closed my eyes
I witnessed passing. As I lifted her
from water, I recall, a spasm
of her backbone jerking. Something flew.

Although I lack religious training
I just crossed myself spontaneously
with silence, prayer-like
and laid her in an aluminium bucket
while I went to fetch a spade.

It's been quite a light and remarkably mild
January afternoon, and as I buried her
there came a lapwing flock that seemed
to seal and clothe the void, and chamber
all the valley for the dead.

Also the single fluting of a moorland curlew
and across the sad expanse
of human carelessness in space,
a shepherd chasing sheep along by motorbike.

I guess I need some angel just to mark
the momentary graces
softly in pencil at the side.

How say true things about the soul?
You spout your secret spirits through the water-hole
    of mossy trough. You shout
your catalogue of elemental streamings,
    Revenant
        of Cloughland, Elf
upon a purple Rose Bay Willow Herb.
    A Green Woodpecker looping lower,
and a Double-Take upon the derelict canal.
        The Iris Depth
in the electric horse's eye. You
    have to give your static to her ecstasy –
    you touch, she shies
Her Equine Majesty and shakes her mane
    and has a canter back around the field before
returning for another vibrant touch.

A sudden tightening of atmosphere
    felt in the ears. Skull ringing
at a faint high pitch.
    The shapes of thought seen moving
    at the speed of change.
An out-house falling in a cloud of dust.

    We can re-use the windows.
    Put them by the wall
    beyond the spring. There
by the dark green growing Elder.

Hello, you failure
       falling hollow
lapwing squealing squeaking whatsoever
You who sever
    on the gale
You waste your breath
    on sins and springs and windows
wishing, willing, a Remission from the moor.

On desert flats I run along
an inner shore, an aural number,
trying every other door. *The state interrogation*
blanks the record out, drawing a furry white noise
through the room.

    A reed rush winds the chordal strings
    A breathing foretold foetal hurt
Strangled, Umbilical, Entangled
in forementioned signs and then gone blank
The sins went black
but for an emblem or an angle: bird wings
in a church. I have given invisible birth to what flew
and now cries on the electric line.

Her blue back glinting in the stone shadow –
I who could panic, get the message, choosing
Equanimity, and then let go.

Expiate the snake out of the chest,
the unforgiven genius of race,
the coffee-cups and egg-stained plates,
the demon of frustrated lethargy about the place –
    Come hooked and landed as a wriggling fury,
mucous feathers drawn out of the mouth,
    the crying outcome of a random rush –
What sex is it? Its fists
    clutch empty air.

Each throb a ring echo of human ecstasy or pain,
astonished in the flood to love
    for crying out loud
above a thorough-going drone, the spasms flatten
and ellipse into the distance
    as a higher ring, the dream of stone,
the waste of generation, spoiled over the world.

Is it dragons, love, or is it doves?
    The couple separate and fuse
    the other side of sleep with darkness
sinking water down the scale a rung or tone
or two. The organ needed to be sacrificed –
    Its tail had grown so long!
    Now there's a lake-child playing safely
    at the gates of sleep. A flush
    of cheeks, and thanks *(afanc* – a water-dragon)
    thanks for the advance, and thanks again.
The place is safe. The inn is filling with
tall tourist stories of arrival.

55
30

Despair, reconciled to Life through Beauty,
Wild Rose, I plucked from Councillor Miss Thorne's
        garden, one Quarter Day, before the dawn:
                An August Gift,
a mist-born being combed and drawn
and funnelled through into oblivion,
                        who missed being born

and passed from shadow into emptiness,
redemption, in a glance
and didn't stall.

        The Progress of The Soul
                a shape
        and I'm made whole

        Wild Winged Life

which must transmute to a possession the
remembrance of its passage through the world
or else
it's Elongated Faces haunting All Along
a lifelong journey.

Better do to witness Truth: by bebop butterfly to
Fullness through a Fullness soul –
        or as the blind from birth recall
their own pre-natal colours, that is,
soul whose all is metaphorical,
        or not at all.

The glamour of her sex arises in the irises
and floats on the aroma of a city air,
a catch, a stimulus, a pleasurable jingle.
Innocence is shaken out, and still glee tingles
    on the streets. The Moon, a daughter,
seeks a father through the further reaches
of the wicked quarter. Eyes light blue like stars
in questioning the Stranger.
    And the glamour of the sexual bewitchment
dawns upon his face. There is a question hidden
here in this my casket. Guess it, *Who are you,*
what is your line, how do you screw? You creature
in nocturnal plumage, have you some young
soul's ordeal come through?
The disillusion dawns upon his face.
The detail scouts for forage.
Hear here grumbling novice voices entering
    the silent square before the sun squeaks
in a fit of shivers,
    a reveille in unhappy valley, or a bugle speaks
its blue untuned dissent. Corporal rises
to attend a consummation in love's fire.
    The glamour dawns
that it was always possible to leave
things still undone and part with grief
the wagons on the road, the baggage-train in flow,
the private nurses
    suppurating sores contracted in the arms of war
and slips into the raw chill morning,
quietly deserted. *Glamour.* Study it no more.

57
28

I have inhabited a silent shining sphere
at the dead end of a line, at the edge
of a vast Oceanic Empire. Here I shall die,
my front room windy as a hallway.

Some futurity, an occupant may hear my scutch,
or sense my line sound in between the battery
of intermittent wind. I'm on my death programme
upon an edge of moor, as baffled as I am
by silence as I am by noise.

Tap-water fills the tub as I feel
with a warmth *Come Home!*
and slip into the welcome bath
and consummately wash and dry. And upon
entering my bedroom find a swirling throng
of small imaginings inhabiting the space
between the window and the mirror –
    switching on the light dispels them
    one and all.

It streams out as the one
bright spot on a black slope.
I resume my line in quietness, *Come Home!*
What was that warm inner explosion of emotion?
Time has turned. I have inhabited
    such mortuary atmosphere.

Sure, it was a sudden shock she gave us
opting out as instantaneously as she did,
knocked unconscious in the rush of spring.
    I can see her at the broken gate –
the waste elf waiting for her in the bluebell glade,
and looking back she's seeing through my eyes
and smiles. The planet's turning,
and the Earth's light raiment radiating Spheroid.

The limping messenger presents the broken wings
to Death with her credentials. Case of essences
and mental records.
The polite guide, with his ring of keys
attends her patiently, at the top of the steps.
    What holds her up on that funicular?
Hello?
      A swallow on the line.
        The hearse rolls to the steps.
The beauty of the earth assumes her in its quickness.
    Ripple of recall, the sweetness
of her girlish laughter on the telephone.

Barked at by dogs she comes out blind
with her eyes wide open.
Coffinned in the planisphere of Sun,
the womb becomes her in this death-conception,
and I can enjoy the pun.
    A jolt and then the carriages move on.
The vicar with her friends and kin comes voicing
interruption: *Let us sing!*

A rush of fresh air,
and the terrace transfigured in starlight –
still a silver dazzle over Blackstone Edge
    transfers as a vessel, shivering, a chalice
cup or ship whose essence is
the pulsing of the eyes at stars, and then it falls
as grace, that rain of starlight, and the cast
of beauty spilt a spell of glamour on the coat of
Earth, *The Illustration of Celestial Love.*

I tap a rush of water off the moor, rinse and wash
a cup and see revealed
my kitchen squalor in the cold night air laid bare.

Despair, except for Starlight
    and the Prayer exhaled. Tonight,
may our elemental conjugation most completely flock
till starlight that is spiritual dribble
from the saturated porch.

That prayer is a mundane wish
to slip into her suite of bliss and place
a pale blue star upon her with the last
bewitching tail-flick of our
Pagan Calendar. The
Dragon and her Mate,
    and we can giggle in the blankets
keeping foetal warmth, and whisper mutual
sidereal excitements.

Whoever said there never was a Spiritual Journey?
Then there was the roofless house
invaded by the nettles –
    mile upon mile of wilderness.

The term of the quest, a vacuous shrine.
Wild water spilling from a broken land-drain.
Shattered glass –
brief blue reflections off the sky.

In fine, the outbuildings look like The Ruins Of Time.
The shed is rotten. The sheep-shelter too far gone.
The shell, a hole within, a shining singing
vacant chamber of the mind,
and round the chimney pots are great
black flapping birds.

    Onward. But where I drift,
dumb randomness,
    the glower
of the sky. The time of year, the day,
the hour.

Time heals all I hope or failing healing kills.
I don't think magic will.

61
24

Discrepant bells
a tone too slow. Old Radio
defunct in shadow.

The railway line closed down
The table overflows into the dark
The newsreel slows
Old gramophone wound down.

What did they bring these children over here for?
Don't they know there's no redress?

The wandering due to helplessness
falls at the gate.
The guards are bored with cards.
There'll be no Restoration now not ever.
Such dumb thumps. *Goodbye!*
I have to leave you stupid
Mumbling in your nameless shining bliss.

You gamble on the bell of one pure tone
There's no redress
Nor has your sorrow any place in timelessness
If shrill is equal to the silver
Full and well, all well and good
There still is no human equivalent available

See these dead children
They are so sweet
They have been mortified.

At the first gateway to silence stands
The Queen of Little Egypt. I
can't follow you down there

    With crashing doors and someone crying *Lord*
How sad is the descent into The Land of Silence
After life had met with such success!

My own death flickers blue between blackcurrant
and pure orange colour tones;
My voice is asking, *Lord*
Am I not adequate a vacancy enough?

I heard my question open long
closed doors on Time
onto a land of headlands, landlords
heads and wells,
    landrovers, stone walls, calling gulls
and glowing beaches,
limewashed dwellings bleached in light.

I saw it closing with a blessed Wishing
    Random joy and very well
in matters Spiritual opening
and closing on the tingling of a bell.

White page of the sunlit court,
the card of day;
blue shadow of my fingers, jack
of my blue heart, the cipher
of eternal stillness, pill
     for an insomniac who's slightly touched
with silly giggliness to find a key –
'I say, could this not fit *the phonebooth* as
a transformation chamber in the brain –
some purlieu musical and hollow – can't you
run it through and just see if it fits?'
                            – it clicks –
The Rush of Life, Transparency, Free Fall
O Lord! Out of Control, down to
a lower down encaverned tone,
     Have I not been reborn?

So *far your echo has been only hollow air*
and some are emblems, zum zum *summer swallows*
of a consciousness in Love. You have made moan,
     Now watch your step. Your war is over.
Only if you can believe
     (interference) *can come again.*
Hello?
     I make believe and dial again.

Hello?

The faintest ghost of steam cheats into air, and
something like a silver tennis-ball of sweat invisibly
escapes over the telephone in rare February weather.
    With wind in the feathers of fire, a starling
on the wire has culled and looped a curlew call
into his chatter.

    Crash of stone and plaster dust, a cloud
of lime and silica drawn in the lungs, the chisel
working on into the coign. In that I heard
        the shadow self whose elf is echo
        holding horses in an empty square:
Their hoof-iron rings on cobble.

O if squeaks could metamorphose, blinding bats
or flapping klaxon laughters of the Earth –
A blackbird thrashing out through holly –
Could I quarrel with my lack of a life's moral?

        Can I come again?
Now watch your step. The fabric mists
and brambles. Barn owl's pastel
pale postmortal coital call

Rings as a tennis-ball a bell, complete she calls you
through the delphic hollows, come you dumb-bell
        half-complete
alone, forlorn
        you hear her flute completely.
Come! hello? how are you? Yes love. Absolutely!

'Be prepared to leave at once' –
Recalling old messages,
just sorting a few things out
as if for the last time.

lest prompter urgencies suggest a quickened heart
with a dark death on the horizon,
turn aside and breathe more easy
once with a sigh in a while.

The pool with pearls of light in what scatters,
I recall her presence,
I keep pointing to the spot,
    Forget the black
wrought iron gates
and catch a glance of water
clouded only in the memory
of her hands cupping it.
The stone wet in the sunlight
where the water spilt.

A Stranger found my heart a door
in an open square.
I watch my child cry in my own mind
raising arms against a memory, in wind
a brass band plays and water sways,
a fountain blots the air.

I take a telephone call in a box
in a time-swept city square.

We seem to be on the edge
of an alien bony scarp
facing the prospect
an inhuman sweep of barrenness.

A train calls out the distances
to exit. Unborn bomb of morning sun.
Explosion of negative light.

The Destroyer holds me blindfold
in a moral ambiguity. Prepare for flight –
They mean to destroy us all –
It has happened before
     on a complacency of scales
          on a cacophony of city streets –
Prepare to leave at once!

    but being helpless I cry help
and try to organise sometimes nothing more
than mirrors furniture and doors
wanting sunlit water sometimes like a thirst
for shapes and signs of peace
     as they come to hand.

Fantastic things were written of
the gnostic phantoms of a sleight of mind.
A dream, only now I understand
the dismissing hand.

67
18

Something Wings
Show me over this Land
Aquila by Name by Talon
Takes me by the Hand.

I eat the knowing of the heart each time I gag
on the road on the rage to the explosion.

A tray of spires is winged on the horizon
With all the music of inheritance.

Psst, Poet, Guide through the Disaster . . . .

I try hard by hand to conform each shape
to the last or latest image passing faster
flighted through the present, as a parent
asking each one of a crowd,
'Have you seen my son or daughter . . . ?'
By the unmistakeable edge of madness
in the eye demanding signs and my
identity can vanish in my business.

Bees are at work in the cells.
Miel. *Michael.* They string
like garlanding the honey passage,
Come Again! for pollen and finale.

The thread through has to be a truth, a link, or else I'm lost and no-one turning in the echo I can turn or call to.

White wash. Shadow sea. My son, my family and me. A soul is tangled up in our impediments of speech. The feathers on the tongue. A stumbling, indefinite and out of reach, a something always on the verge of sounding wrong.

Demon of The Deep. The channel clear. The quarrelling of birds out on the breakers. Blip of radio. The snuffle sound of him asleep. Now to my eyes appear the figures with fresh garments and like jewel clothes. Sea death. The Pearl in my Romantic Chest. The family sleep-walking on an August shore appear and disappear. My mother moves between me and the door, insomniac with cigarettes and too much coffee, and the worry, all her grand-children, all day, waved back and forth.

He's here: Pip of My Trunk, the Apple of My Eye, My Snake and Progeny. For him I stake the Heart of the Beast Romance. I talk to his dead mother coolly in the dark night, of our prospects, of a refuge from the deep dimensions of magnetic power, looking through the windows of the sky, over the sea, to see her.
Night sea cry. Indigo. *Are you sure?*
I swear upon this coast of many colours. Demon Cross and Dawn of Pearl, the Seal and Kiss of Sleep:
Goodbye Forever!

Jupiter, Apollo, Venus,
Sealing the visible world with these three
demons, Sky, Sun, Earth, the works,
     sweet honey words,
the wax of being.

Bees purr in the ears
the poison of the void
     A cornucopia
the trumpet pouring in the woodland strain
The Person of The Word. Good Lord!

this Penis isn't even Jesus, just
the pantheist expansion of a personal experience.
A Clarion and Female Christ
     A Flower for the Clerk of Works
Lord of The Yard
     The Patriarch
     the bruiser in a flurry
     Father of a brood of feathers
     Cock of all his doings

in the sunlight. O Ye Gods
authentic pastoral absurd
     in pagan
green and blue and gold.

Assimilate me, drone ye
voices of the humdrum day! nay
let me even be thy image-keeper – I
have doings in this business kingdom.
    Heartbeat flutters. Silver bells
    sound palpably absurd.
    Floating down, caught napping
lucent threads out of the air. The webs
and filaments, the finer, fairer hairs.

A second brood of swallows form a flying school
and wobble, wheeling, kiss, and feed in flight.
And I'm up to my eyes in love's adrenalin
    The violet blue in thistle flowers
    The plum in heather blooms.

The cow's mouth crops the thistle flower down.
The flurry of the floral sublimate, swallowed
as supper, slips into the oral gloom without alarm.
The seal of celibacy broken in my soul,
a swollen sorrow globes and glows, vacuity in flow.
All bluely coos the dove. A timeless tumult or
a tuneless swelling, groans fallacious love. Her
eyelids flutter like some flying thing about
the blossoms of the broom, the rowan berries
and the pink wild rose.
    All wilderness
thy garden grows
    and seeds over the tomb.

71
14

Is it not consciousness of love
the birds migrate in? Old
Mechanical-Organic quarrels.

     Predatory wings above my shoulders. Weird.

A dread of terns takes flight out from
the drear vast wastes of icy paranoiac silence
of magnetic fields. A flurry of the nerves
of earth intelligence. Acute, sheer white
and nightless, even as the solar or the soul of
light. A polar midnight.

Try this door into the atmosphere tonight,
And is there no reply? The kinless stranger
with his collar up against the wind walks on
his death programme. No signs except
the Day Original stands flapping by the rowan
like a raven flag. Vacuity.
A barometric fall.

Blackberry eyes. Bleak sky. Black dots
and spots of rain.

Is not the planet earth a living being?
Why? Why not? The colony debating
dizzy levels. The departing issue
of respective nesting morals,

72

13

I caught her eye once when the lid was closing
and it sounded like a doom.
    I blanch and flinch
and Earth and all her train whirr through
to drink at the flash brink.

Slowly traffic flows with flowers. All her life
she had inhabited Romance and sought with me the
fellowship of swallows as they'd fleet over the
goblinish industrial expanse.

Wet eyelashes. The light like wings.
    A dragonfly over the water
by the silver birches in her glance.
A moon-like smile come through the palor
    of the morning blue. A spectre
through the cloth. *Oh Christ!* All Nature's Orphic.
    Hierarchies appear diffuse –
class over class, with crashing jars
of porcelain and glass.

A burst of clapping from the parlour
Tears in the front room
And laughing on the stairs
The doorbell sounding funny
Loudly soon
The lid closes over
And it sounded like *Gone Down!*
into a deeper room.

Gaunt Shape haunting the moor,
Moss-troopers of an old forgetfulness
approach the border-stone and cross

the centre in the fifth dimension,
Swear an Oath, *Mother of God!*
Cross my lost heart and vote and hope to die.

Since Christmas these Romantic Christians
march to find the spring of an objective ecstasy –
a living nothing. *Bloody Mary!* or
some other love. Their banners
rippling fire. The ripping yarns. The web
and feud of blood.

Come Easter all my magic pirates choose retirement
        and the family romance is shelved
with a well slightly Irish wish.
        'You saw the chalice in Orion, did you? – do
mind how you go.'

I hear the train sound rushing well below
The star streams pulse
I wash my face and wish
The Phoenix of recurrent virtue,
Love and Verdure, on my doorstep,
Brightness, mirroring a merriment, *for
Many Lifetimes,* if I heard it right.

11

Enter Fool, who rings a bell.
     Open your cans of larks and laughter, Spring
to Balance, baffled in enchantment, dafter
than The King of Egypt's only daughter. Tintin-
nabulating on his Golden Branch to make a music
of intelligence, intentionally sexual, to rapture her,
The Princess in The Prime of Venus, ah
so she gasps her ghost, Pulchrissima, into a
Quality of Air, her throne is bared, a sepulchre
beyond the stars, and lovely after words to share
with her sheer girlishness.

I must be soft to court this astral shape.
A tattered vagrant leaving holes in wake.
An animal upon the clear road to the stars,
seeking the silver everlasting,
taking lunch out in the sunshine, chiming
with the cap and bells of all celestial learning,
tokens of a mating yearning,
rhyming the disasters of a broken heart.

Clog-iron on cobble. Song sounds madder each
Pace-egging spring:
     'Twas I that fought the fiery dragon
       And brought it to the slaughter
     And by these means I won
       The King of Egypt's daughter.
In my book, rhyme's the signal of a pagan daftness.

75
10

Elder, in The Shadow
    of the Face of Venus,
Guarded by The Keeper of the Abyss –
Bitch, Mater Dolorosa, Ellen,
Eileen, Helena . . .

the circle of the pool has long been broken;
several shrill wraiths, the elder witches
of wild waste escaped
the fate of fire and mutilation.

Now what fruits behind the gate?
A waterfall.
Who holds me by the halter but
a short stream or a vague dwarf?

Cypress, under Saturn,
Avenue of Yew
in graveyard ruins,
Silent gongs that tell the ever-green way,
Times, and long regret, and causeway sadnesses.
    Undress in satin
    guided to zips for nectar
buzzing necrophiliac, a mutual belonging
sexual succession. Spit
into the wind across burnt waste,
For generations, No Respite!

Crow caw in the quiet evening
    from the leafless branches of a dying elm.
A rogue wind blustering the little starlings
    displays like a weasel and then disappears.
Kiddies playing in the classic sandpit
    of a seaport city park kick sand
up in the air –
    it swirls and anticlimacteric falls
    in crystal trails.

Under cranes and gantries,
gaunt shapes of the warehouses and the wharf,
a great slave-trading Empire caving in –
the yawning stairs, and tenements collapsing.
Broken wells, drains, webs of care and welfare.
Gnashings from the pulpit of a Militant Heart.
A frisson crackling on Atlantic Radio,
blip blip blip, in static air.

    A dracula, come to the edifice,
    the shape of the approaching storm, with
    an unconscionable yawn.

The thunder-enfilade to drumroll
rumbles through aetheric thickness.

Spider, in the sunlit stone-shadow
of the empty offices of old Trade Maritime
perfects her net.

77
08

An old man in the Market Hall
    with the brush of a fox;
A woman passing with her hat
    a lapwing crest;
From *The Labyrinth of The World*
    to the Paradise of The Heart
Each uterine original is bound
    to eccentricity and torment
till it find its tonic in the octave of
    a key star of the soul born of its own.

I met the emanation of a school of thought myself one time, when I was clothed in purple and scarlet and gold, with all my edges frayed or flared and flapping, hitch-hiking one April way back on the old Colchester Road, in 1969, when I was burning in the sense of being on my own. I took myself to be a devotee of light, attempting to escape The Empire, when I came before *The Living Phoenix,* face to being in the world itself a mirror, stepped out of my crystal stupor, and I swear I sang out what had all the makings of just one pure tone. And soon I'm shaking in the afterdazes of the star of Venus, rare green light in rare green weather, fits of rainbows, colour, cloud and hailstones.

    I try to calm the dancing panic. Quiet air deep in the ear, letting doves fly out of the shadowy barn, despite the still hysterias that madly lap a lake.

    A white van of the water-board arrived
    to take me to a place of safety
    if there is any.

Privatized, enclosed, with lawns and car-keys,
door-keys, mortgages and curtains, babies, washing,
angels, crashes and divorces –
Processes of natural selection,

    I'm the servant of this world, a spectre
of the black economy, filling my bucket
at the garden tap. The gush jangles the drum –
    cement has maimed its tone.
Spray spangles from my trowel at an angle
glossing to distinction blue
    forget-me-nots.

Free-thinking.   Guardian Wings
    a touch of this
and I go cuckoo through a rainbow screen,
the dream-contagion spreading with a shower of rain,
the damp greening the stone,
a flapping crow up at the window –
    Muses, can you tell the story through me? –
I'm not in control.

Raking out in ancient masonry
    the pick releases native
ancestors and ghosts
in gusts of active dust.
My pointing closes up the holes.

79
06

I saw The Raven in a cloak of Bloody Law
turn and declare
This witness by his own works stands accused
of torment and confusion
He has been the agent of his own delusion
Out of his own mouth sable plumes.

There was a falling down out of the blue
There was a house with many glinting windows
There was an angel falling from the roof
onto the tongue, I testify
in feathered fear. I try to speak the truth.

I saw the arguments come out of his mouth
He was in his Luciferic Grandeur
A resplendent Rat
His body shaking, making fly
Out of the mouth of Hell, a fright of bats;
Or like a cat takes prey, he spat
and though he didn't shriek or cry
There was some terrible burning at the ends of his speech
Which were frayed with the smell of discord.

This should have been a proof that it should flow from
flutters in the stomach-pit of love, that it should bloom out
of the mouth a pure white dove, and fly over the coloured
streaming fabric of the Power in Time, through outrage
to the haven, fort and harmless pleasure found in foolish
rhyme.

Go down into this hollow tree: a stair-well, all its
landings lit for Christmas, underneath The Vault of
Stars, a chandelier. The Calendar of Years. The many
rooms with fires. Go down with torches blazing to the
mossy cellar of The Prison of This World. In one room
there's a reading in The House of Life, The Tree of
Trees, The Throne, The Kabbalistic Crystal. One room
opens on a conference of dreams, another on Imaginary
Railway Systems, Stations of The Cross, called strangely
Manchester, London, Sheffield, Liverpool, Leeds.

Each way are options such as Poetry (English),
Computer Explorations, Structural Reaction, Mysticism
Defended, Personal Defeat Denied. There are passages
and passages of Psychoanalysis, and there's a party in
hysteria upstairs.

I found my number here with all the structure
luminous. My door, the narrative of how I came here as
The Wounded Soldier with a broken heart, by witches
intervention – weird – I have a Princess on The Cards –
Opening in wonder on these present lights.

I run upstairs in this dream of dreams,
There's a gap that opens on the steps,
The way into the depth of death,
The chasm of my own ineptitude,
The mystery of England in decay.

Blank blank
Pan! Pan! Pan! Pan!

A vacillation in the birch leaves
of the magic world of synaesthetic
naturally arising naturally blending
harmonies of sound being absorbed
in whistling undersides of leaves --

A car comes to the wilderness gate
LOW FLYING JET ATTACKS
the portals of the ear,
an aura takes on sudden eeriness,
concealed and ceased.

The leaves slowly resume their
panoramic solemn converse;
flutters of silver laughter
chance out in brave profusion. Wind
stirs the swirling river pool.

The nature being not to have an ending
other than
there is in the imagination such a one
as lives in wavers
and someone
who attacks the peace.

Fire of demolition timber crackles in the night.
Human noise evaporates across the waste. Beyond
all living. Fleet to enter into moonlight. Deaf
and disconnect. The breath that goes to greet
white outline ghost whose landscape . . .
    I elocute over the fire while water
falls into a trough. A tilly-lamp reflects upon
the surface of the thought. The glitter with the black
star of obliteration at its core. A galaxy in water

For our company of animals who thirst to drink
and surely make some noise before we die
to help to send the soul to pass into
perhaps no light at all, and nothing stop
the ring vibrating here for all eternity, each thing
vacating each thing for infinity for which
      wellwishers flute futility above the fall.

My heart stops beating with these wings.
A shadow flits and flickers on the wall
and enters company, in spirit
         I loquate
    we come the purest just
    the object of some atmosphere.

The stranger breezes of the rushy wilderness
filling the air of fire with whispers of more mystical
arrival. Fire falling to dust
    and ash before our eyes.

What if the loading soul take on its purity as a plurality
of focal modes, of modal folk, of fickle morals in a
muddled way – upon a pelting by-lane when *The Road of
Life* made sorrowful sense, and then a blackbird's song
pools brilliant violet upon the wet and so dissolves my
quibble. I am lured into a sheltered silent glade. I find
the elf within myself and glitter in among the gladed
insects. *Michael, this is a malfettled model.*

If all such doors into that space prove false, I fall into
the wind and whistle what's already siren atmosphere
political. *Deep Centuries.* The need to rehabilitate survival
and experience myself against the leanest desert.
Absolutely Soul survives I say against philosophers and
allcomers. Let wishing well be ritual, Aquila wedding to
Alanna is the immaterial made all one flesh, a willing
union of millions, without the chapel building, one in
the baptismal water, one in running babble, I can hear
my valley tone of bell.

Hands together; eyes closed. Fingers unite. I see a
dark enclosed fore-shadowed scene. The glower on the
fell, and tumbling clouds. A drum beats the retreat of
glamour – On Culloden field? What? *Kilmichael?* I am
trembling. I've been acting strangely. Out there just a
turnstone plover plucking catches on a desert shore.
I tried a door and found this only open: Beauty in the
shellfish Life, however terribly acute falls down into the
dark the dreadful feathered sacrificial pun.

Writing in a nearly lightless loft,
my candle lost, my last two matches spent.
Dark flux over the woodstove, skylight luminosity –
Corona Borealis. And a draught of air
    takes shape around the trapdoor,
wafting with the scent of hay, – *Come to me!*
Conjured out of nothing: Love
is meant to be loved to be sane, if only
Phoenix multiply my days.

Fingers untie the blind.
I'm home and standing in my doorway
as I wash my face with a wet white flannel
drink a cordial of spring-water and lime
and wish the day,
    reflecting on the valley tone of bell,
the couple of our sexual scufflings
in the natural dark, I wish the light,
and it's the skirling lark
vaulting her spectrous speech into the sky –
like that I wish to hear The Phoenix sing
    through my beginning heart of wind and blues,
along a memory of avenue, a querying
Revolt against The Zodiac,
Attacking Keys
    leads the excruciating silver
into shiver till
    the practice is perfected
metaphor

                and to continually sing,

00
00

This work derives its origin in contradiction between conviction of the priority of vatic, inspired, and oracular practices, which, in my case, despite pride, run to the bloody awful *and,* my actual practice of re-writing and by some instinctive principles transforming everything I've written, with some sacred exceptions, over twenty years.

It seems I was fabricating a book to blend exceptions with their background in a way that might divulge, even to myself, instinctive principles underlying my shift of drift.

I think of it, pretentiously enough, as a sequence of improvisations upon double-sonnets, within a musically classical, almost palindromic whole.

The pagination is a decoration of this process. From front to back there is a development of life in time; from back to front an adventure in fiction and abstraction; from the centre to the peripheries, two versions of the illustration of an impulse.

The proposition is that all may be resolved in an art whose meaning is objectified in the moment of appearance of number.

84, in my intention, stands for an idea which I discovered for myself. It's what I found I had to say since I couldn't escape the word *soul.*

Aleethia,
or,
How our Nature
Represents The Truth
(1990/1994/2006)

I.i. /1
These ears remember silent lapses
in the utter length of sound.
　　　These eyes
see from a source in voices flowing to
the waste and soil-pipes through
the drain down under ground.

Evacuated chamber. Flushed.
Another vacancy is filled.
　　　Tacit Eternity! All its investment lost.
Accounts of the exchange lie unreturned.

But the lark raises bones to a post in the wind
and sings its clean particulars of heart
　　　　　to the blue pasture.

Me, Ah Me! I feel inept and empty,
valueless, a living hollow full of holes;
a watch that stopped, whose living time is up,
　　　I stop to watch the sister echo
come to sip the flashing stars of water.
　　　slipping into an escape.

Farewell thou then, *The Education of The Heart,*
　　　for thou has been *The Thing Itself.*
Remember me, and aye
　　　we shall be with you in the long
Predicament.

I.ii. /2
The shadow of the snake is being broken
in the exhalation of an individual
as heartfelt, from the lungs
and for all living things.

Slow down then.
    So then down
through hollow colourless and yawning chasms
goes young so and so
    with thunder pressuring his ears
and he has had it up to here
in a miasma of umbrageous glue.

He goes to enter intercourse with silence
    there to read the glass globes
of his soul's own education
    into rings and bands of an arising sound.

Ah, *Fooled You*
    Calls the Curlew
Through an Air-Blue Phrase:
These Days the Earth Is Hollow
    Like a Maze.
A Cloud is Liquefied before the Eyes
And in Reflection Sky is Spectralized,

The Wind Plays a White Noise.

I.iii. /3
The heart preferred this should be heard:
Here empty emptiness into this emptiness:
An education of the heart is its inheritance.

The King is Dead. One certain morning
on the margin of recall I found the curtains
of a soul undrawn.

The traffic stopped
along the black main road.
Appalling bells re-pealed.
My own heart beats
and no illumination is revealed

but lightless absence
oscillates by vacillation into scintillant-like love,
as though *Erosis Rose*
a single chasing tonic mode. Glass. Water.
Startled Physic. Spirit
        falling through the core beyond Recall.

The Queen grins in the green of trees. She is
The She-Hostess of Ululation. I'd been drowned
in wordless speech,
slaked, choked, and smothered down
in moister seed. Suds trace at snail pace to
the trice-ring and the soil.

I made my way into the middle
        of a slow sad tale. A trail
of all my missing things discarded on the way.

I.iv. /4

The tale I am about to tell is the awfully dumb long story
of *Peony*. She it was (you will remember it was she) who
grew and grew, and she had grown to globe the empire
with her wombic irriguity. She used her willing then to
spread the swelling of our irises along the twisting lake
that issues in a serpentine and river snake. It was she
who was lost in some shrogg of thin woods.

I want to see a breeze deploy across a sea of such
simplicities as these, across a sea of trees.

And she did not consent to her perdition. Happen,
it is we who shall be ushered, feathered in the issue,
entering a tintinnabulation at the whisper ringing in the
regular elapse, the inner weathering and water of the
heart.

She may be masculine as me; but She is *She!*
She issues through the room with glasses;
She gleams with semen and the meaning of the heart;
She seems at night upon the street to glisten,
    a ghost in the heart of stillness.

Cowed, as cold, though cored, and something cawed
with cries of fulmination I can listen
to the beat inside the humming quiet of the night,
the murmur of a television set switched off,
the rainfall, and the filamenting hiss or whisper
from the gritstone sill drawn fine toward a dawn.

It seems the psychic wounds are being healed within
    the mostly metaphorical.

II.i. /5.
But I am slow, for I am aboriginally bonehead:
Speaking as an animal, I'm liable to be quite miffed
by startling little fluttering haphazards
of a philosophic wind, however well its ministries
are well-umbrella'd by the welkin, in diminished chords,
whose minstrelsy is mincered through the cylinders
        and issues in a dish of such publicity as this.

See where I'm dumb, I feel excluded
on all sides. My hands go frantic
        on the glass of mime.
My inward loss of sound sounds bloody awful
in an atmosphere of vacancy and poisoned wells,
and I can hear them bloody drums behind the door.

Let be, and they become as tumblers
at the ready for the spring.

Invite them down to drink
the wettest gel, the glinting rill,
and let them let themselves to swell
within the eye-grin glitter.

        Wholly Well
they swell into The World, and disappear
into The Air, becoming Globes
blown through The Wilderness.
        They let themselves
be educated there, be thrilled
in the transparence, shrill as I am
come dumb ignoramus to a wordless speech.

II.ii. /6

The spirit bride of light by now is much besmirched. In
her condition, she's unreachable. She left these emblems,
hoping these might teach who seeks to find through
ambiguities to true remorse. And, vacillating at her
door, I think how rich a speech, and sounding fatuous,
and sounding chamberous, the comic star would sound
— like wood sound, do you hear, with owls — I would
my seed be uncontaminate; I would my hands were
clean.

How come small hopes deflated flopped
had come to muffled nothing, moaning small
untenable tones? How came I
in my infancy to take the rush
to intercourse with silence, shaded
in the green of leaves, and really meaning
to be strung out now, and sung in Endless Time?

But *Oh!* Me and my spirit bride
are forced of course and drawn
        into the overflow of Living Force.

Then by analogy an infant took
the private road into the inward of the night
and found the inner ocean, and the sounding shore
where waters pour like poor forever, surely
through the hollow core.

II.iii./7
How well the hollow rushing sounds
through shells of shadow emptiness!

The can of worms empties A Century
rebounding down the sandstone shaft
            to Zero down below.

The Shining Grimace. In the Taciturnity
There Can Be, Under Saturn, No Return.
I have tenacity, I swear. But please let go.

And then a speech-like noise deploys, deploys
about the keep of reticence for weeks,
petitioning, or undermining little verbals,
sappers of the nameless faith of mine.

I mean to keep the nameless face
although I have abandoned faith
in wasted ground. I must maintain the pace
of breath and find the place I left her, where
she heard alone the singing stone.

Here I kept my Patience. Here I was chilled
on The Silver Road. *Aleethia!* I sight my Soul
Misunderstanding. *She!* She was pregnant
with Showers of Air. *Aleethia,* I sighed;
My Soul I know
            Not Understanding.

II.iv. /8.

Touching dewpoint of the story, there's devotion to the
ghostless, the sidereal and decomposing world. This has
to disregard the episode of capture by the heartless echo-
shadow, that was stimulus-response, and the condition
of a one-note conscious and unmodulated tone, and all
extruded texture into single abstract lifelessness.

But yet it touches this, this Earth my sleeping
place, by breath at peace with Christmassy but slightly
christless stars. Hence I'm elected to a rounding globe
through sheer devotion, at a touch: the entry of the
figure of The Perfect Stranger,
water flashing stars all afternoon.

Then I went out through ecstasy as quasi-evangelical
for some absofuckingbeautiful ablution, wetness, up
below the hawthorn, high on uninhabitable land, in
daylight shadow, fleeting one among the water-verbals at
the portal, watching others washing, issuing and taking
grave prescriptions, wishing each the other well into the
air where living bubbles go chimerical, hysterical with
chemical and unachieved ambition.

OK, Michael, for thee and thy Ambition,
to come to want the blue grace of the source
to empty and exempt remorse, for once
or twice while quelling imps impertinent,
I'm thinking of expulsion, in a trice-ring grin
and, in the grinning, wince.

III.i. /9.
An ullet shoots from the moist heart of the wood.
And whiter noises water at the ford.
And why no withy willows?

But now, what outbreaks on the air
but popping ears,
    But Sir,
Lay Down Your Arms! This Is The Time,
And I Am Here!

And, lacking all my eloquence of tongue
Olim Ab Ovo to the fruit of misdemeanour:
That shall be A Placeless Throne, A Calendar,
A Squealing Wheel, The Colander, A Sieve,
a broken vessel with the silver liquid spilt therefrom
or settled as a tillylamp upon a pool
reflecting flashes while the stars are all
extinguished as expired. And I look up
as one who'd been long years exposed,
abased upon a brink. I see the vacancy, a trap
a tap, a flowing gas:
    I am escaping suffocation in a lack of light,
and in the night I hear the trains of living signals.

The bristle rose to pitch. A whistle flooded all the intervals adrift,
but I had heard a hidden door that isn't there had opened on a
thunderous aurora, aviary with hidden splendour in the signal
promises to rush, flap, and from offing rise into the other outline
shape of the Throne of Rings, through Shade resounding
    with glad reddening of heart.

III.ii./10
Come over here. I came to hear, *Too Late!*
The Bell of Anima has been repealed!
I came to overhear in fact
        its minstrelsy has now been discontinued.

And the dirty river sounds down inward
in the valley dark at midnight
in the precinct of the throne
        like of abandoned rings.

I take my education in the wash, run through the inner mind, and
pee at a rainwater downpipe from the troughing.

And as I please to piss I watch the ghost of a throne arise into an
umbra of dark starlit blue. So many stars, and all my wellness
sprung unwarranted into a trough as fresh, stone, cold.

A flute evokes the barguest from the copse.
Then comes the storm. The storm has come
with newborn globes in risen wind:

It is *My Peony* that *Has Been Killed.*
Is that a bleach ejaculation, or some seal that's spilled?
Obliterate O Echolalia!
        Have pity on
the animal I am a male, forsaken
in the willing failure of an old undoctored tale.

III.iii./11.

O Phoca Vitulina! Sounding of the Fruit of Seas,
you lay your belly uppermost, to be wiped
by the towelling breeze. And, may it please you,
Please *Allow* my willing blubbers now
I am come naked, clouded, troubled and unwell.
Regard or *Disregard* this wild pump eaten by disease that bleeds.
Within these bounds, *Redeem*
this mottled angle of the trees. The breezing breathes.
    The hope of feeling seasonal succeeds.

And I had come thus far with my sandwich in a dream to where
the gate clicked open onto Ocean Nothing: all the sky went
strange, and I stepped down to deafness, sounding sundry like an
almost silent sea. The cows and clouds went with the darkening
mechanical. A blank light stayed. The heavy traffic passes on a
glass-like plane of sound.
    Now out on the horizon there's a range of something dark
volcanics. Down these paths accompany The Stranger. Look how
we can depersonify ourselves, whilst passing variously through a
range of doors of speech.
    And Where Is Your Shadow Now?

This is my shadow here. I know this valley. We are on the edge of
something deep. And, do you not exist, I'll take you, take you on,
and fold you in the sad case by my seat, before I fall asleep within
my overcoat.
    A warehouse silence over muffled water opens from a loading
bay out onto fog of only Open Ocean,
    but it seals my sleep.

III.iv./12.

Upon these steps of stone with how sad eyes a serpent sang his abstract scale so strangely sweet and charming in the changing mode, that all the sour and sordid settlement had seemed far better ordered than my un-lulled senses ever could accept it was. Upon these steps of stone I lunch upon these phrases:

Let *The Inner Journey of the Soul* be something that the sliming Serpent swallows Whole; and, Let *The Spirit*, an excited feline fire, be blown. There is this job to do. I have this cross to stretch across a canvas waste, whose emptiness hides gates onto the water falling into shapes of ice. I have to stretch across the hollow core, unfenced, unbounded, dangerous, and dropping down below into a blue and siren aura, dumb and dump, ordure on order, and gone bang and dung.

I burrow down into the mound. I have to bind the found-out image of the dragon-self, self-fathered by the child, to find and free the wilder bride of space. For now an arrogating power has come, has cast and slid the wormy feeling of the heart across the sentences. It looks like we are in for stony-sounding centuries.

Now, looking down, I see the smoking hall of silence, grey so dim. It could be taken for a sanatorium for some stage of its distance. I seem to sort of see it in a filmy dream of sodium, streetlit with dismal orange. Now my ear is drummed with drear and self-absorbed drills of forgiveness.

I can hear the scale, though, singing:
Look In Here!

IV.i./13.
Look in here: at the illuminated intersection.
Shadow haunts the hollow cylinder
whose way had once been stars and water.

Shadow, having lost the inner will to heal
had lately grated like a squeaking wheel,
and just went cuckoo through an echo shed.

And Shadow, like a shadow, now undresses
to his loose and ragged pants to face the worst.
All his intelligence is in his negligence.
He might slip easily into that cavity of years.

This cavity lies open in a hall of air, and here
the shadow rests, a guest of certain seabird spirits,
secret, though they fly about in open air.

I think the shadow knows his only way is by the
ghosts of passage opening throughout the senses.

Taking breath, the shadow takes a leading edge
along a length of crumbling cliff.

Then *Follow!* speaks some seepage from the
shadow slipping through the ill-lit woods
and livid water-shallows,
I Shall Take You (Who are you?)
I Shall Break You
in *The Simulacrum of a Drinking Party.*
I Shall Wake You.
        Sipping purity of coldness
on an April night of frost.

IV.ii./14.
O Silver Star! *Thou Name*
and Archetype of Patience,
        Stay!
Such things are being done
bang in my heart,

while emanations infiltrate the moonlight
on a rhododendron-overgrown estate,
Domain of No-one, Ghost of Time
who gave two hoots out from the gate,
whose prey has died
        in cypress shade
in this nocturnal state,

while out beyond the headland
in a blind wind, water rains
upon the well below the tide.

IV.iii./15.

Before the hall contracted to a lightless corridor, the wraith must make escape, abandoning the echo shadow, bonded, banded, bounded in the ring of time.

And, having flown, it finds the clouds are colour mixed across dark texture in the seasons of the wind.

The wraith reasons that this must be the shape of the Corporeal Mate. She had been left inside The Shell of Nameless Fate, or is it Faith?

He hears the shouts of children drifting out to the grass.

The grass sheep ate.

Beyond the third gate to the long strath
a begging wind accosts the cars on-horning up the pass.
At last she has been taken up and ushered through
the educated globes by paths
through withies
to the steepest bluff:
Now Look Awake! Now Look Across
the Sky to Valley Floor. The Moon
is Bright. Can You not see a Cross?

She is the silver in the clouds. She is *Aleethia*,
not solid but unsullied,
loved by the full-ness of nothing at all.
She's hallowed, not not Not Allowed.

She's shimmering, all still within
a traffic crowd. All stillness loud. Black ink the land,
the laund. And oranges and lemons in the sky beyond.
And, on the sea, with boats and islands, blue in silver:
all the stillness of the sound.

IV.iv./16.
Opening
a fourth square gate:
      four bars:
the blue:

Sometimes I Get So Worried

then, as now,
upon a traffic, or a green, or desert island,
(and there has to be a crossing,
and there has to be a link,
a causeway,
and a bridge that sings,)

that sings with purity,
that sings with dissonance
at which, where if I slip,
where if I make my great mistake,
the soul makes use of unsurprising wings,
takes flight and makes
migratory escape.

Something's Recrudescence through to its Effulgence

Also known as

**The Calder Cloughs,
Four Poems, and
Three of My Chasms, and A Fourth
(1993)**

Sothfastness

If I'd stayn sothfast in admiring love
while others changed and left a new address
I still would not admit I'd been bereft of soth
nor call unknown on anything this way:

Come something come, supply me some new way
to find the steps of water falling for a memory.
Come give me melody, the line entendrilled
locking to the key. Give me a line,
the line a life describes, however general
or generous your terms may be:

> *Old Sally in The Willows*
>   *She's a thing of Cans.*
> *Oh Shit! She says, You shy at we*
>   *who smile like summer suns.*

This shong I think it should be sung Pianoforte.
I am drinking like a donkey when I plonk
into *The Glum Deep Lumb*. And this is a thing
in shadow, which I call
No, No, Go Not Through Arcady.
            Attend.

I came unstuck at Castle Carr
and trailed through mumble rhododendrons
       mumble mumble
ornate stone. When I got to the steps
I came unstuck. What could I have done?

One windy day I came home sick
and chanced on *Sothfastness*. I read it in a book.
I lay and watched the clouds display themselves
across the panes of glass between the mullions,
keying Sothfastness into Mental Recurrence,
and hearing cloughwater slipping the sill of grit
I sleep tonight between a duvet and a pale blue sheet.

Sothfast comes like a soft gong. Oh no.
No good. I've done the something wrong.

On my return I beheld the fall
enraptured by the gale. I faced
damp flaps of flannel wind. And I
say to my heart I say, *Be still and eat*
thy bloody handkerchief no longer. Know
it wasn't thee I was minded to want done away with.
    Look, the wish is still held in the willows
where I made it, and the space it holds is
empty as a quiet day is of all else
besides itself.

The sea has reached me in ensuing dreams
with a motor-boat starting its petrol engine
and the sail flap of a cutter, stranded
in the swash unanchored,
washing up in the sink below the road.

The shoal sounds dead in this noise encompass,
turning to look down channel,
the valley a deep road of air.

I must not be stranded here but rise
with swilling gutters.

I was larking on my own up on Walton Edge
hearing within the bang and ding of doings
down at Scotland Delph, the wind
where its shining shakes the trickle shallows
over pillicules of quartzy grit. It's nice,
but still I come to grief, and wince,
ebb long drawn out, the upturned keel
of run-aground romance, no doubt,
shown through the layers of a repeated dream,
in clear quartz through transparent water,
words become my thought,
    I've given her offence;
There's No Forgiveness; and
    There's Nothing For It.

When April air turned coldly greenish gelid;
when the corpse of shadow had been buried
        in the garden
there was nothing to be sothfast to but death,
and any innocence is so much wasted breath.

The corpse of shadow is quite livid:
That's my Angel now down-feathered,
suffocated, suffering below;
not the corpse of shadow but a creature of light,
though as yet it's in an unreverbified state,
it is The Phœnix *when it comes to life.*
You knew you had your pair of witnesses
in your Continual Song,
        (it stopped)
and you again went wrong.
But I can't sing
Something in August greenish jelly midnight air,
it wouldn't come out right.

I was in the garden delph and pissed
against a slender willow trunk. Why I'd been
blamed and blasted on my toilet,
      bludgeoned with a mug, and kicked
on the kitchen floor, I think I'd
rather never know; nor with what moods
to do me with she took her pleasures.
I just walked about a living dead thing,
over ridges, into valleys,
      with a havoc in my head.

That could be just the day the demon came
like something in the post.
I dare not wish to die.
      There is no keening
and no oracles are worked unseen,
but I thought *the soth,*
      to the willow trunk
and the dampened earth
as I wished for this one last verse:

I feel proud, like proved, in thinking this:
I have established sothfast in the grounds beyond belief,
and I'll tell you this: It took some doing,
like there were all hard edges to be left or evenned
to the ground, and then thick swamps
and seemingly unfinished wrongs.

But suddenly this spring I seem to be
wholeheartedly admitting and admiring beauty,
that it is something,
and come whatever follows on.

The Green Woodpecker

INTRODUCTION

The Cuckoo-Thunder broke on Spring Bank Brink
and scattered urinaceous droppings of a sudden
coming green. The zephyr
caught into a meteoric shape
here culminates, brings these, and leaves
a spectral virid trail
of amber glass and greenish vitrine.

I suppose these are what the poets call
the harbingers or heralds, now the scene is set
for the re-introduction of a shy fair sun
with mist-cum-shine, through mellow glass
to finding something in the water.

I think it sunk within my thoughtstream,
something seen, come blurring in the flow.

I've been up on the brink again this spring,
and I write while the crockery
piles too high in the sink.

I have the use of a garden delph.
    It was here I decided to sow the seed
of my this-life's ghost of discontent.
    I think you have to do this in deep dream.

The deepest of these dreams I know so far
    is this: I felt a feathering
within the air around me, and I turned and said,
    Aquila, is that you?

It was a figure in the chronicles of this
    Return to Poetry, beginning when
a willow branch had scraped the roof
    of a green-painted aluminium stranded caravan.
There I am writing, thick
        in the instant heat of bottled gas.
It's late at night. I stop and doff
    my shoes and trousers, feeling soft
and pent in comfortable underpants.

What next I saw was a figure for
the number of four globes
enceinturing an orifice,
pavilioned with feathery hands
in a receding-in-perspective hall
'that disappeared into a sky
with minute bouts of turbulence for clouds.

I think it then was evening, though my doubts accrue,
my doubts had somehow calmed me through.
I looked ahead and smiled and said,
Alanna, is that you?

Is that not daft enough? Then look at this.
There was a corpse laid flat
on the fork-lift truck of these beseeching hands,
and only just this side of the fence of final silence
and I want to know
how long is this floating in eternity for?

Then she came up the road from pure vacation
bearing sheaves of news of our own local
apocatastrophe, as though we might
with glue restore the star-tree's greening lights.

But there was no thematic miracle
but one long marital disaster.
She had finished physical
in forays climaxing in incandescent rage, and I
had fallen between stools on the floor.

Then a long-delayed shock as her glance deteriorates.
I think it's sinking, and I think
The Comic made A Mess of Things
with Good Intentions, standing soaked
in a fleet of like flooding sands
in socks and just these underpants.

Then I took the rough track into a badly-overhung glade,
that gave the shadow canopy. I went by bluebells to
the river hole. And if I saw myself I'd wonder
what on earth I had in mind. A Ghost.

It was like the mood of a croaking daw
and a length of rope, in darkness
in the very early morning.
You can see the hanged man's landing
in a loud wind along a very foul shore.

It was also since I'd got
some buttered shock electric news
from the post and dropped
the marmalade across the toast
and spluttered choking at the cost.

On a walk I have come in the dusk
like a bus to a terminus. Shaking my motor,
and shivering, on with the lights.

Here you can smell the effluvial stream
from the mill, while the nightshift sweats
        over cotton. The dusk falls through
the cliff of woods
        to the fluminous swirling bend.
Like a line sent on an errand
it will come back empty-handed in the rain.

It could have been just here
that the light first stabbed the heart,
and kept on stabbing
while the stream fell deeper into trees,
and reached the bridge by the railwayline,
as though wanting to scream.

Once only, at the back of the van
at the end of the train
there was a woman vanguard
disappearing with a placard reading
SPECTRAL FREEDOM, held across her chest
and she had no face.

Again there was a check shirt flapping
in a warm August wind, when
the clouds dip down to a brown
horizon of mud, and the ribs of a wreck
protrude through the wide ebb flat.

I think of shrimp-like movements in my brain synapses
at the opening of flood. And soon there's some
wet spinning whirlwind thing impending.

I am left calm in the bay
    of an imaginary weather-window
dreaming being left aloft
    in a breeches buoy
when it snapped
    over vastly-photographed cliffs.

I have been known to suffer troughs
of the phenomena of atmosphere, when if
I wanted witnesses, then all I heard
were gasping whispers of the co-conspirators,
but you know me, I could be trapped
in the deepest pit, and still I'd see
the stars in daytime, thinking these
are my terrific angels
aiming down at me.

THE GREEN WOODPECKER

Looking forward, chopping kindling,
bright but from the disenchantment
curiously wrong, I laugh out loud
long outlawed laughs or songlike lengths
o' larks o' mercy, saying thanks I think
for animation generates or generation animates
the place of light, and then I think
the living ones perform as moving places,
all the young ones being young at once,
Huzza! along the edge belong
triumphant lapwings up in arms.

Within the fabrication of a life
a sudden breath takes like a kite,
a cold cloud warming rises to a height
along the edge and that evaporates
like laughs at a disaster.

Then it comes. Ephemeral Pontificate!
Picus Viridis! Updraughted
with a farfetched laughing cry
has me you know like reconciled
consoled and no less silly.

My Chasms

It's many years since I was shown
the crystal singing in the stone
and given feeling felt the breeze
curl up exhausted in the trees
and then came home alert and heard
the single singing of a bird
above the droning sounding-dome
of Burnley Road,

but I've since been up to the green hawthorn
where it issues in the shales of gritstone
and heard the curlew flute, and then felt stranger
chilled in dismay, an unwell child in danger.

Indigo floats and flashes on the green
show spectral scales of snake-shadow
left in a slack the ebb had sunk below
and in the thunderflash, again Indigo.

And I made up this awful line:
Now all my hope is like an abscess drawn.
And I think the abyss was mine.

I remember where this was.
It was somewhere.
It was somewhere sundered in the sound ring band
and kept, and then withheld
by the gills, it emits an acheing wail
into the blueness.

There's a street of snow and darkness from the train
of my *Spectral Freedom,*
and a voice that says, *It may be indeed
that the snake has eaten Anima, but so what?
It was always a nothing-to-shout-about life from the start.*

I think the snake had only eaten
nothing that is never given
but had hidden Anima within.

The moon is whitening the river.
Shadows pull upstream like gradely worms.
And then a bird comes stepping from the gastric space,
    comes up the steps like from an empty guest room
        Turning In Ascension
           Through The Hollow Into Light.

The wind removes with a laughing clap of seizure,
shears me off all but a glimpse impression
of an eggborn flying thing drawn in
the furnace of a mill, like once
I was born almost but spontaneously aborted.

From the shadow face of a moss-cleft rock
deep in the clough, the voice of daft vacuity:

Strangled Feathers. Water Swelling.

These are my chasms

sounding through my home below the road.

I saw the figure once
when the bank's fields were green.
A car along the back
removes it in the noise.
I heard a clear glass moan.

Could it have been my witness? No.
Our breathing now agrees,
        it sounds mellifluous
throughout a shoal-white sea
        through which the she I mean
takes breath and swims and breathes
        upon the sheen.

You watch the leaves as backdrop, and
you see the wind careening through the trees.

Out through my door
        I follow on to knock
my ashpan on the terrace wall
        and go back in.

Are You Still Eating Shadow? No.

She walked right through me
just as though she were a ghost
and I the precincts of a moonlit
sleeping town.

　　She came down
to the shadows on the shallows by the bridge
and these are too my chasms.

A planet shines through my window in
to the white cube of my room.
It makes of it a sphere
that's seeming fathomless.

My stove heats water. An electric pump
distributes it around the house.

I can live without my ghosts.

There are them birds as flirt.
In fact there is a company of cocks and hens,
and I'm with them
refluttering over all our waterfalls
that dash between the trees in unison:

My Chasms.

A Fourth
(The Bridge that Sings *Over Effulgence*)

An Ouselhen upon the willow
clamours so the listening world
will grant the claimed attention
    on the collective and reflective points
of a global auricular sphere
    the song in tumbling, in response
to this alerted person
    and I have been heard, and I am
hearing, more cleanly, and I am calmed
in her melodic lines, and I clear my throat
and I try to speak to say

I have heard in my heart thy throat
in its utterance make, like note to note,
like mate to mate, like soul to soul,
such calls as make my drawing breath
to let befountainously out the warbles
of my celebration of for thee
my gracious losing marbles,
    Venus, my
Coronaberis, Thou
    Christina

in response and answer;
and our natural history, how, I didn't know
for the hen as it is for the cock
how feathered somethings rising
in the song as now, as, aye,
my cock bird's burgeoning.

I left her for an hour between two birches
overlooking the deep blackness of Loch Ness,
while I slipped higher up into birchwood
looking for the face of Mater Dolorosa
on a boulder, that I'd seen years before
in a wooden glade.

And when I found it there the sense of
        fallen hope, in a space
of blown-down trees was like a pastoral
        and picture-natural of faithlessness,
misery, and the always-legendary knowledge
        of more youthful folly, and me
decked with weeds, wildflowers, sorrow,
        lost.

And again, under a full moon, it was this
my heart had heard hard hoofbeat of a deer
from off the wide bog-myrtle flat
as crisis like a clap of atmosphere,
a test that, failed, would let loose that despair
whose ghost is ever lost upon some given junction.

And it brings my own attention to my chances
of success as outcome, and I shine my
gosh how weakened light upon my heart's
green livid fitting wildwood crisis. There she is
        among the birches, settled in the gentle flaps
of strips of canvas hanging from a birchen branch,
and curling in the flips of playful breeze.

She begins her speech at a high tuneful pitch
        in a song that rises, as the walking lapwing
ascending the field.
        My song when it comes comes
all heartdrums and pips like a linnet
        in spattering bits, and spheres
as the sprayed explosive.
        But her song, ah,
it is the native motive of my take-off votive:
        she electrifies my quest, and I
can testify I sense myself more dignified
and must have done with suffering
the slow space suffocation, with the ghost
Despair, that mournful haunter of the
bathroom door; the screeches of
the howlet from the holly on
the brink at night; such piercing brooding
into my own breast, as I had used to do.

For the song is our love has come off
        in the same green garden delph
as had been my place of burial
        for guardian angels,
and seen me renounce
        the slightest claim to inspiration;
but the spirit was raised
        and the desperate ghost was laid
where we came off, as when and once
        among these rowans, furze and roses.

I had opened my casement. Reflection cast
an angled new scatter of streetlights
out across the heatwave late at night.

I had mistaken my nasal breath
        on the pillow for a thunderstorm
and then my heartbeat for her footsteps, but
I heard a cough, and there is someone female
along the terrace, reaching down in bright
red, in lintel bulkhead bright white,
in red bright summer clothes reaching down
beside the rosebush for the key beneath the stone:
        It's she with whom
the brilliance and puff and plume of love came off
        in the haw and wicken haugh.

And going glow through stream bridges
        there's a flow.
And there's a fresh glad outcry
of refreshment, Goodness knows
the lucky beings looking out to blooming lilac
among rowanflower, mayblossom, broom,
lots of long dripping wet grass,
        and the wet grass moths,
through to roses and kisses in practice
        poetic as wings. *Trust me,*
thou wilt be suited, sounding just a touch stupid
with my mouth half open, now, I'd admiringly sing.

The shadow of that happy cry
    I can identify,
the shadow of that exclamation
    from the bower in hawthorn
was the screech of alarm from the shadow
    being laid
upon the brink of explanation.

We were thrilling out
like ousels in the rush
    and leafy brush, as two thrush
up in the hills as on full
    flood tide.

So at last, buffed and baffled
by laughing, all Calderdale above,
fields and cloughs, I am pleased
for myself, and my own vocation
to be like anyone on pure vacation.

I believe this is love, huff and breath,
with the feathery I, and the feathery thou,
flapping flap flap flapping, enough.

The quiet points, ignition of a car
that yet creates a turbulence of air
that lifts a pigeon and a piece of paper
briefly into spaces there, they flutter
down through spaces in the Piece Hall square,
where she's erecting scaffolding, and multitudes
of mental flowerings lift through my corner
of stone-shadow:
                    She is my love,
        and that fluttering,
the pigeon settles down on cobble setts,
the whole quadrangle wobbles
        and returns to form this square
of clearest space around the soul's glass sphere.

The piece they'll play is the Midsummer Dream
and she does Quince, if I may say
exquisitely researched upon my local self,
which makes me laugh with love for our affair

which has been written through the rain
and rowanflowers of the following year
while she lives in the glare
of the railway at Crewe, near the station
in adjacent, what must once have been the
railway workers' dwellings, in a small cube room
filled with the keen bright atmosphere of her.

Eyes raising
      feathery and serpentine
the sight
      from stone shadow,
the Spirit its Resurgence.
      The *thou* the dignified,
      the signified in feathers,
      the fount of endlessness song;
      the *thou*, some common thing
      to cock and hen.

Thou spinning wish or spiralling,
the shine, the rough dovetailing
      with the ringing gongs,
and like a burst of laughter,
lyrical, poetical, and beautiful,
colourful, one of those songs
was like crystalline liquid,
and I think it was the oracle itself
that made me laugh to see the poet
with his penis putting like the crown
of pompous folly like a head-dress
on himself. But I liked that
Venus Christina bit best.
It was she who sang most cleanly,
Silver hammers, silver tongues.

At last I am puffed on the edge of this
    self-celebratory comic foolishness, wired
on vocal struts across toward
    what trips me, self-upstaged
by puritan reaction, who, with quick humiliation
silencing the universal silliness, returns
upon the clear bliss world and would the pure
woodland tone maintain, of contemplation
    self-explained.

On offer is an instance of
    encompassing phenomena.
I play the prime, the native and exemplum
    witness to the song of ringing spirit
endlessness again: *Cloud Wonder*—
Any eggborn infant's had its head in.
Scents!—The welling out blue float, blue lilac flight,
    the halcyonic something on the water brights
        the heart and both the heart's adjacent
blood-lymphatic swellings wing and fan
    upon the gasp of laughing.

"If, through eleventh hour, a lifeboat seems to bob
    off a threatened rock," I was struggling with such lines as
might maintain the rhymes and senses of
    an earlier personal draft, but no such luck.
        But look on how things are.
Now, from the doorstep of my dwelling I can stand
to render puffs as from a flowered and exploded
pod or star:
    My thanks. Love blessed my lungs.

Three springs I've breathed with *something's*
       recrudescence through to its effulgence. Now I finish off this
formal immaterial event, just shuddering this
       side of the acceptance of the fence of full hawthorn
effulgence and the scent, *Mayblossom on my*
       heart, the woodland cloughs and the adjoining fields'
luxuriance.

The same bright particular star that's constant to
       the shapes I hear, the sphere that's the idea
of planet music brights, lets love-mist breathe upon
       the house of apple-friendship, bites
into the aura of the moon.
                                   Myself I think
       I do prefer the *wish for,* find it purer
that the *prayer for,* through the distillation of
       internal proof:
                            The offered something
spinning to the apex or the crown of a performance
       wherein shadow sheds itself, and something
rectified directs itself to dance through flux
       and all sorts of efflorescent and excessive
finishing in floriance, as I do on my own
       internal border of *in tune.*
                                   May I
as any hold to one such air and happen
       though the polyphonic comic's gone so far,
gone far, *gone far,* walk out
       to find refreshment in the wind and *find*
the spring's again a tonic.
                            Mine's an *F.*

Bauble (Burble)

Poems written for A Whole Bauble
(1994, with revisions up to 2006)

A Lubrick Loosed

It's like a sly evasive wit. It's like a shy reflection on a set of cellar steps. It's like saliva on the lips. It's like a highlight to the eye; it's like a lubrick or a trick. It twists the tongue into itself as it escapes.

I should have loved to lure its source of likeness in, to organise the making of a threnody for when it's gone. I could have thrilled to sense it shiver as it takes the bait. But as it spilled its reputation surreptitiously it left a trace, a blank, a tip, a bit of luck. It gave the slip.

I read it once and swallowed my acceptance of the verdict and the sentence: To be taken down by hollow lingual alleys and be bound to serve a term of time in dispute and in disrespect, then to be smothered in expiry in the matrix muff of nothing minus happiness, and any skin thrown in the lake of dreary slime that's drying to a bed of crusted flakes.

A shadow in the shedding light that slowly showed descending stone, I sniffed the fungal passage must effect arising from the trap for soil and waste below the cellar steps. It must affect it to be dead. It should be buried. As obsequy, let it be said:

How lavish of its offices it offered silken thread, and yet how tacitly and well it kept the spell of secrecy alive within the cell, not letting any ghoul of imputation or the ghost of a suspicion ever touch or taint a hair — if it had any — of its silver head — but put a subtle finger to the lips, blinked as an imp, emitted squeaks, and with a crooked limb it shut its lid.

Spriggan Fair

I.

Up to a shriek and yielding, the excess gave let
to bleating at the throat. The field was rank.
You knew it needed to be mowed. I had a spriggan
threatening to run amok. I'm not conceding
what was owed. Expressly it was being booked
for being bloody cropped. It shot that shout
so loud that the machinery had stopped.

Expanding crowns up to a loaf of steam
and bottoms out. A spell explodes in bleeps
and bits of soundless broken flak. I had been
suffering exacerbated bitterness, remanufacturing
my fractured wing, the gripping throttle —
you'll excuse me as I crack the bottle, but the pain
came as I saw them waddle out across the lea
with all their fine mud-flinging tackle, spreading
what-is-it, the freight of their fertility
until they're spent up on the thwaites —
I count to three.

The cloud is held up on the pass.
The cost of reaping drops.
The shining watercourses weeping
       cannot stop.

Again, with cattle on the aftermath, let's say
I heard a song about a snake who ate an apple
on a bale of hay. Okay, I take it I can happen
wait for what'll ripen in the latter days with
ruddy globes of wicken and the sanguine may.

2.
A sleeeper's leaping double takes
a folk-shape of the spirit outing
to the fields of fair reality.

All readily an early gaggle clamp
        and couple scaffolding to raise a catafalque
and plank for the performers.

Tonal blenders to the tonic test
and practise feeling pitches. Other men
are stringing canvas bloats
into a steady ripple, airing hopes
for the acoustics and a mellow day.

There's a double with standing
in strands of gourds and trinkets
when a rosebush of a sudden gust has let
her petals flood across the flags.

Later on there's a misunderstanding
as trouble is raised in among the people
to be reaped and cut and dropped
for Ancient Dobbin to clop off with in a box.

Abated at a tap in washing up
I had felt for my partner being taken
in feeling, joshed and doffed.

I'll say I love
and do not scorn to josh the dolly
while the boggart's cleared off.

3.

The bush cropped at the neck. The pouch back-
pocketed. Hold on the grip while sobbing ebbs.
Then cut and rob the dead.

It eases as you had it off. With one more squeeze
the lid was flipped, the tufted duck took flight,
the laughing stopped, and stiff and white
the corpse had rattled off an audit of
remaining numbness as another crossed
the pass in smoke between the strands
        of ghostly ash.

The toff had spoken
with an aspen trepidation: You have caught me
in a sense in some perplexity for cash.
This is my holiday. Let long debts pass.

You kept a bottle up your skirt and hit him
such a smash as hurt and left him landed
in a lake of liquid spirit, bits of rock
        and broken glass.

Folk are mocking his deceased demand
for better service in the courting of his class:
the sporting ring, the country interest at last.
One clash. Dead fright. Too loud. All over.

Vibration can't reflect nor shine increase it
in its passage out in shape in pandemonics
touching once upon the time to come,
and there's his knocking from inside the coffin.

4.
We're in the book, a double bill to top
at The Pavilion. When the rubber men have scratched,
outstretched, squealed off to pop,
and all the mummers' props despatched,
    we're on.

Tugged by a fan of strings, a hand delivers each
a spriggan to a bunch of imps.
    Another hand digs in a pouch to fetch
up change. Eyes speak assent. A crescent brow. Let go
in one long derepressant hiss,
    I'm missing you.
The big one from the crown dividing
into filaments of inexplicable division,
multiplicities of never-fine-enough
    to fill a pinhole.

So decided we must say no blether
but to say together *Spirit Deicided*
in the rout in twine: the one to shadow blight
of loathing foiled; the other grew revolting
in advance and shrank fastidious
into a nicer neat recoil. So though
we came to scorn enjoyment of
enjoined performance, this was not before
we claimed the making of a new thesaurus:

I speak of a fervent performance,
and a certain spirit form.
    What did you spend such time in Celtic Folklore
and The Fairies for?
    Called Spriggan Fair.

Schooling

Trauma Bell

Bristle at a shrill pea-whistle, an alarming warning to beware
of The Invisible as buzzing swarms coil belling out through
an embrasure, thrilling to a boil. I'm learning, *Thistle, Rose and
Thorn*. I wrote my way through school in fervent scrolls of plume.
One day the forks have snagged me, had me sagging at the knees.
Bonnet beset by bees. It was a fraught and fractious morning
when I brought a tray of teas onto the sands. I had been rattled
out of doors with flying saucers coming at me from the hall.

Calm down to school. I had forgot my work. But then I'd run
up to a railing where I can't recall. A cold silver spoon down the
back of the neck, and it stops. How old are you? The bell is for
your close.

Weak fingers touching on a noose. A Crow. A Carrion. A
Crown of stars pops up out of my heart's bestartlement. Some
something had been carried off, but in a bustle and the crowd
frequence was turning blue. An infant faints in the regard
profound. Unkindly spirits of the waste-ground ring to watch it
drown.

I just bobbed up with this bill for duck and I'm off back down.
I got but bruised afflight. My curls are frizzling now on yonder
brazier. I got lumps in the throat and burns down there. I got an
oar full on the ear, one on the bonce and shat my pantaloons. It's
one right merry-go-round down there. A fair carousal. Now I'm
much in need of fresh apparel and appraisal.

Was it fake arousal of The Saviour? But it's getting late. They
only let me out on good behaviour.

A Suicide

A suicide, before she viewed me bleakly as a shading to
the prospect of her dark success took me aside, and
showed me these: her *Steps*, her *Rope*, her *Trap*. She
thought we might be sharing these, but I was horrified.
The shawl was ripped. The flood run wide.

    I cast us off as she was lifting with the tide
and soon she died.

    The rest is sadly flapping flannel. These are
slides she showed one of me coldly stealing
from the pool. The stole was ripped off incidentally, a
stoat caught in its net. You see she drowned, but
something floats, and licks itself mid-channel,
silver wet.

    Like a great lapse orb the engine globes up
close to sense. Let glitter quell out on an even ebb,
with petals blown into the meant immense.

    But, use some gumption, Goodness Knows,
the winter snows are almost burying the heather.
You are in some foul distemper since you had to swear on
oath you never ever drew even a single
sliver off the figure of her dancing in the mirror.
All her corpse was drawn out on the banks of one great
living river, moony, limp and damp, and enveloped in
slime.

    Let her go then protesting, aquatic as ever,
gone and flown, wherever and with all her younglings
grown. At home I run a tub and sink into it my
unbending knees. My knees my own, but me
unknown, who steeps in mottled light regarding steam.
Who can unknot a subtle gut and briefly nod through
this one's own oblation to the drain, then double up,
pull up the plug, and glibly quit, like file the dream.

A Hawk, A Horn, A Stranding Bay
A hawk, a horn, a stranding bay, a daylight shriek
and one night-landing. One right raucous aura
smoking from the pool. Stock still
    white hands and face
betray no breath. She couldn't waft a petal
in a moonlit glass fiasco but was sundered
    in the dumb unsound.

Flying at night, and falling, in the failing light
to land on losing ground. The green glass grate,
    the glaze and scrape of tireless wheels
on flats of ice. The traps are set,
the livid pitch of pressed vice, the silken cord
unliving down in liquid dormant lies.

It was young bobbin bullied bubbled cobble-bitumen.
His arrow flared off. The gargoyle gargled and,
evacuating spat. A thing dead in a sack.
Dig it in bracken waste. Go bury it up slack.

There was a headstrong child came once to fling
a bucket full of flower, grapefruit, urine, slops
out on the ebb, who bends
    to swill the bucket out, and rattles back
up sandy shelf and steps
and disappears into a shaded door.

Pure Pause before he reappears
with knife and plate
of bloody fish-heads for appalling seagulls.

The Subject
The subject, pure and simple, missed its footing
and fell off the cliff. The King is Dead.
And all the traffic stopped on Blackburn Road.
That was King George the Last.

The subject lay off school, with 'flu, in bed.

Two minutes' silence.

There was ample time
to view the ghouls awaiting with a raft
beside the lakeside waste to draught
the corpse across the silted moss.

The subject is discovered counting off
blue usages of word abuse. The same
who came to water shining in the pines.
That moment is a point at source. I call it Elfin
Norse. Step up and ring the scales. And then
the nymph with lubricant for skin rolls up
in waterproofs, predicting storm.

But this is merely winsome whine,
a peevish wince, and then
        Light split the pine
through every last particular
hypnotic shine. Sheer absolution.

At Peace Dear Heart Strange Minds
Are Draughting Out Thy Human Constitution.

Dissemble
Dissemble. The dissenting chorus lacks a quorum broad
enough to bury this consensus in. The Anglicans, for all
their clangour hang their heads
and try pretending prayer. Some solemn doctors
dock the tail that had a power to speak
and heal, to freak and to anneal with flame
    and seal the perturbation.

Here you catch me prying as a sleuth into the
so-called silence; gouging with a penknife
in the sacred wood. Winking under a hood.
A predatory beauty understood.

There was a mill above the tumbling where
the brook was forced between the dark brick walls,
below great blank blanched windows.

Effluent pipes thunder on the cinder slag.
The unspoiled world stays unrevealed, the soil
unreeled, uncoiled, unravelled
as the lightning struck. The purple glows.
Discard the line that tries to save the soul.

There was a type who tried to train a tube
through to his room. That line was never used.
The fork had found out where to crack.
The glade turns mauve and blanks in the unseen.

The spirit with a tail upon the scuttle turned and spoke
such squeals of utter dullness, gruesomely
as in a vice. The very devil got my goat to bend the knee
and make more eloquent the grammar
    of a stern rebuttal.

A Slow Voice

A slow voice calls the losing numbers, missing buttons,
blanks and numbness, yawning in fatigue at desks,
behind the counters. Some of these and some of this, and
this unease makes like that wasp trapped in a bottle.
There's a voice and then the throttle opened
through the epiglottis. Clocking on
    and slowly longer off. That's quite a lot.

Curls of hair blow out where nothing matters.
See she sways beneath the leaves in windlessness
and doesn't breathe. Beside her laps what-is-it in
evaporated mist.

They brought me out in dripping trees.
I cannot say that in this valley we have all been
happy but *They brought me out in dripping trees.*

Flickering light. Traumatic ghouling. Then
a line of sheds led to a lantern light, a slatestone
shield, a gang of men. Dream-trauma needs retooling.

I came up of my own unmended need.
I have been strengthening my fingers, clawing
at the wire fretting, where they caught me
wishing ill down at the waters' meetings.
Willingly I'm getting on through school.
I do find less and less attraction to the fatal pitch.

What got chokes in the throat got drawn out
on a long uncoiling rope of gut. I'd got
to be the Tosspot, emulating, showing off
the water-serpent, but awoken by two
    heavy-handed slaps on the back.

Ovidian Slips

Ovidian Slips
Ovidian Slips and Nothing More.
    I had come to the lips
of The Sybilline River. What
        had I come to the sybilline river for?

I had come to the pool out of tune as fœtid,
quavering too loud, and stilted on my legs I stood,
a would-be one, immensely proud
but failing to admit that it's defeated
and in need of such a course
        or metamorphosis as this.

He's been the spitting image of his dissertation:
How It Is, the seminal identity must acquiesce
in its displacement if it dare to face and bear the weight's
        repeated onslaughts on the state of grace.

But I had come here sickened privately within
        my own insistent fiction, not to gain
publicity and risk disgrace, nor seek redress.

And, breathing on the glass, I see how aqueous
the essence of a living is, and place these lips
        on the breast of this, and feel the hiss
of The Sybilline Source, and see how messed
the edges of my orders are. I seem to stay for ages
in a scented state, amused:
        The Lake Has Floral Borders,
while I'm shaken to the core.

The Unloosable *Pun on a Ford*
I've come to the river. I'm sounding the horn.
A mist-breath rises in the field of vision,
glistening. The cry I heard:
high-pitched, self-desolating.

I might have known my goose was cooked.
I came this way before. Again this year
I have been cuckolded some more.
I've had my feelings badly torn,
        my feathers burnt,
and I've been pigeonholed in darkness
with bewildered doves.
I don't think nothings learnt.

Liquidity through shallow falls. But I was
frighted at ignition of *The Flaming River*,
barking mad. I saw the shape it left
die back as quiet more like tidal falls,
the tail between the legs, ashamed.
I came here to be shorn and sleeping wait
the horn, the comb and scissors of return.

Still Here?

I dreamed I'd been stillborn
when I was woken by a goose arising
whole and giddy through the pool and gone
with flocks I might have known of like
        migrating souls.

The More Terrible Slips
I lie inside without control of my
wide-rolling eyes. I've seen me go
so clouded I obscured the skies.
But when this grace alights upon my face
I cry *Goodbye Complicity, Goodbye Surprise*
before an unexpected sword descends
to interrupt us, shredding instincts
into slivers in the grass.

Am I not satisfied? Time flies;
the evening flocks. It looks so late.

A shriven forfeit as a rule may be accepted if
        it's naked and alive.
That could be my certificate and I'm
to have it framed before her grace and heard
in audience before the echo dies.
Her Grace is like the bitter taste
of blankness in the eyes,
and I'm shown up as shaken but no wiser
        for my faking lies.

Let slip....
The day she spiralled in the midges
as a swallow dives across the clouded surface,
        set against:
Let Slip The Knot: A Craven Nuisance tries,
        trussed to a tree to die; *subsumed with:*
flaring in the cry, and so accepted or rejected
as recurrence/no recurrence to the lips of fate;
sets up together: such a sort of dialectic as
        the sexual spirit, and a sleight of mind.

The Lucent School
The blush reversed, the blood was drained,
    a gulp at first had helped me blank out what
I'd done, and blank again at why I'd come
to school in tears without the terms
    I had deliberately rehearsed.

By the claw in the back of my neck I was seized
and fetched. I come to have the pressure eased,
the claw removed, the poison drawn,
        and for the blessing
to be drenched in one aspersion of the horn.

With a goose, with a rush and a wild return
a fluency came fooling through the water-hole.
The shallow glitters sounds and shoals. A wispish soul
inclines to slip into the pool. Stripped to its lips
it calls a school of waving males and females
ululating all its cry's display: It wails
        It's willing.

The pool was fully solipsism, but so full
of others some of whom were sporting far
more nakedly than I, who shades his eyes
to find in some particulars
of ocular response *a love all over.*
With the splash of an unqualified explosion
and a shrilling larynx
        I had waded in.

A Book of Odds

(a.)
Is that you, Proteus, or Mother Goose,
    or else the *Dream Soul Self*
who has come to a bourne,
that is The River Ocean, very very wide

whose eyes gaze out upon the waste of incarnations,
wet blasts in the blowing wind, as darkness falls.

She leans over a parapet like a
    Solicitous Great Nurse.
She haunts all history of verse.
Her dark winds hound the moon,
and as they leap
    all sorts of things break loose,
the hand-rail comes away,
and there's a flap, and sudden falling
    to the world below.

Flap flap. Reflap.
A fleet of flake-bright ghosts float high across
the night's obsidian. A strange light cast
around the shoulders of a coast
    The flagrance of the host.

She left me in the twilight on my toilet,
in some sheltered lapping, or like
pillowed in the hull.
    I can't say truly if she were a Goose
or he were Gander. Surely she were
    Grand Dame Nature
in such Amplitude and Grandeur.

(b.)
Screened in the rain. Balloons are hopeless.
She stands in her underthings, and vents
    her ample breasts.
The streetlight in damp leaves plants blurring
    shadow-prints upon plump flesh.
He drops and steps from cotton pants
    and they stand face to face.

She brought him soon to suffer one great
    smashing star-come, at her hand let loose
in strings, directed by her stabbing fist,
nigh-perfect in velocity and zest
across her vast ballooning breasts: her best
stab just her last one when
    he howsyourfathered out to space.

Head over ears, the hapless bauble drops
into a walled-in hollow, pit with falling props.
Tristesse of lust remarked upon the face,
grace and disgrace. The laughing dog,
a slobberchops droops toward sleep,
    depleted.
The wallpaper so grey and ghostly white
    in failing light.
They snore together through the night.

(c.)
To the hawthorn tree in the high rough field
came the equivalent of refugee:
and it's only full of birds.

So much effulgence, it just isn't true.
Emprickled under canopy,
I loved particularly she I called
      Prunella Modularis, I could blow her
feathers into sky for poetry.
She laid no eggs. I fathered only words.
A few grew up untrue and never flew.

(**d.**)
A Kestrel falling on a slide
removes its presence from before my eyes.
Its wing-shadow on grass below lopes idly
looking like a saddened
    lorn black raggy
on the picking-field of a starling-band.

Read my thought: *not damaged*
but deranged, as when I married.

Kestrel shadow forms a goblet
on the glass-green field
before it shapes itself into a hand
that turns and waves itself away.

I think it sort of takes events
I somehow sort of thought
I sought the thought of thanks
one might give quickly to the flit of augury
as if accepting what it meant.

(e.)
We drank a potion of the magic pudding
and felt fast appreciation of a shining ring
in which arrived a cartoon mangled klaxon
    language omnibus
with baggy clowns and tumbling buskers
on the sand all afternoon. Those pantaloons!

The whole familiar menagerie appeared late in the day.
My Goose: A carping tone of brain flouts up
a goat-like shape of ragged scarlet flame
    flares up to spout: The pinhole spirit
of an evanescent flagrance,
speckled wildfire expirations, vanishing in froth.

I just burst into tears
    at the sight of Vipers Bugloss
but I laughed as Comic Spirit
    flew up flue
with Good Old Mother Goose.

(f.)
Violet spittle-juice, cursed through the teeth.
Tin ear infinitude.
A curl of rope looped over absent ears.

—Someone had found them, wandering out there
and brought them back to ask
Whose Ears Are These?

Wisteria had scribbled over brickwork.

(g.)
Viola catgut. Scarlet squeaks.
    Viola catgut snaps.
Look on the bright side. I must shield my eyes,
count worms in shadow as the corpse subsides,
as, starved of love, deprived.

The melancholic puddle gives off intermittent
grumps and bubble-rings. Then something
gave a puzzled look into the keep
of deep Eternity as it went down.

I lose the goals I fail to keep: One down and deeply
lost in thought among the trodden daisies, just as she
burst through the mist in shorts to slip one past
my unprepared defences. Two down on the worn
settee. She raised her knees to show the rose
original to me.

I have been irked in feeling cartwheel squealings
of a rodent in the field—Do you not want the Love
that is a basin for my offered blood,
my magic pudding? The blackboard chalk
squeaked crying scribble, raked and wreaked
then snap. And that's viola catgut lax, at last relapsed.

I just sink back and scratch the slate
with fingernails in wet sand at the slack.
The sky stays overcast, a dull slate grey.
And it reminds me of a passing pain
that in the memory of life remains.

Playschool

This is me, I'm sure this time, being beguiled,
uncovered, shown the sun as undefiled,
tip over-spilling golden rose across a bed
of pure white cloud. A flouncing spread floats from
the crown. We're on another dark dome station,
watching it advance to parturition to complete the
dawn. Look over the exfoliation. This is
me whose prickled skin erupts. My fear is being
taken in to meet preposterous originals
of metamorphosis. If that is me he must
be ringing in alarm, come novice to be
plumed and primed and to be tried by Fortune.
So Good Luck this morning winding down where
sound is due to be resumed. It may be me,
the plot has found among the trees, in cloud low down,
the sodden ground, damp hillflank.

One draws a wondrous froth of course off through
the pump that is the heart's in fact of life:
such bubble-notes from stone sink in a field
or risen fountain in the centre of an abstract square
go effervescent with a needless squeal against a
painless needle. Call me headless, call me heedless, of
such superfluities as this that fists itself
into a spray of tearful leaves.

The hawk unhoodwinked. Leaping strings. What's it to
be? The woodwinds pipe disorchestration
into streamery. That's disallowed. I cannot
swallow such a message as this is. And is this
    to be me?

Idle fingers waddle for a moment on the stops.
The *string* or *stream* across the *steps*. The scene might
open inwardly to melody, but never
tell you where it goes. *As thou art bound,*
the story goes, *then take them steps below.*
I will agree I'm not too young to overdo,
⠀⠀⠀nor old to rebegin.

There are silver birches out along the railwayline.
Not so good for wood's umbrella from the rain.
A humble-bee had quickly tucked itself among
the pollens in a foxglove-bell. I want to touch
upon the love that lives within our blood.
I'm hearing sharply warbling birdsong alarmingly
⠀⠀⠀close in the sodden wood.

What seeing, in the swirling bowl of turmoil,
seems like being seen by someone? I don't know, unless
it's something in the way the flow is combed,
across the blown-out crowd of turning crows,
against a sky of *Spectral Iris*, or else something
in the mystery of languages as well as
⠀⠀⠀*English Rose.*

And still I'm cold, a stuffy nose. I breathe and sneeze,
and cross to seal the chest, and close the hole.
Well bless or blame me, there's a square right here.
A square of blue filled with the coils of air.
The flying tendrils of invisible phenomena
that form a shell-shape, dulcetly re-opening to let
them flow, and dulcetly re-close.
⠀⠀⠀May I reclothe?

Reclothe: the whole arena in a flood of light.
The mellow meadow blue, the cranesbill and the wild
sanguine geranium, the yellow flag, the briar rose.

If this is me, I itch all over. My discomfort grows.
If that's a square it looks uneven, and if these
are understandings, I don't know. I have to go
back home to bathe and sleep or change my clothes.

Regarding though the bowl of turmoil, and the cloud
of turning crows: The picture is of all the specks
in extra-spectral, the bespectacled spectator
to the spectacle, blown up in air and through
into an aftermath with fern-like fronds in all-
surrounding fog. I think the fronds might mean the f
in *Signifier* as it snakes along.

Cheap resonance from devastated shopping-centres.
Cheap revenance: The Demon, *Froth-in-Spats*.
Cheap reference: wheeled out, a trolley or cheap pram that
overspills with disembodied limbs.
This scenery of pantomime seems insecure.

I count to five, the number of the spikinesses
sneaking in down by the rotten gate.

The show is this: I'll show you just one set
of the hysteric shapes, enough to show
their usefulness in mass hypnotics.
They'll perform before an audience for silence
and the slides. But you must promise that you'll not
      believe me if I'm telling lies.

You see before you such a blank. Dead silence.
Silenced. Numb. The dumb show. Then a rope
around the corpse in trees. A work of art.
It's critical. It's cracked.

They speak of labial saliva, sibilant abuse.
I called for truce, which was accepted as they whisked
me through to worse than words.
All further fuming failed to fend off the attacks.
I got worked up about against for instance Jacques Lacan,
Portillo, and my banding for The Council Tax.

To all intents and purposes I'm gone, and then
The Snake Within The Wings appears to calm
the fraught, and flatter winning my consent
to play a part, the very central and important role
of that which has to take the blame delivered
by the women for the rape.

Have you not ever had the silly feeling
when you're being gulled that what is charming
you is just your look of being eager to be pleased?

And yes with eyes, this snake with cuffs of frills around the
hands, stage-manager, whose way
of walking chimes with thrills works like a charm
and I say, *Yes, With All My Heart.*

And this is where integrity of ways
were redividing. In that sudden
disenchantment I had felt the rubber
of a disused condom.
        And I fell apart.

Later, down the garden path I could be shown
the maps and proofs that there are no unimplicated
sources in this evil stew we call the earth.
Indeed, a feathered pride in this respect is
reprehensible, that comedy colludes
in an acceptance of *The Friendly Fiend*; expounds
the dreaming of the soul, in the expiring little spasms
in the grass, contracting gasps, where even odd
earthworms may represent *the breathing of the earth*.

The other way, back *redividing*, went by *beauty*
and caught sight of *Pan!* across the valley
stepping from a dark brown space between the trees,
and has me running from
    The Blue Snake
walking like a man.

And as and when I ran, I ran and ran and ran
after the instant Pan had vanished in the wild,
And running sung sing-song:

    I'll Pay My Dues to Ideal Truth
    dressed up as Princess Alice
    if it's all the same to you
    while yet I can.

Through gracious ratios I ran. Can anyone outrun
a talisman and end before the race began? I ran
all rainy day, and came out in, with, on
the lorn and ragged thing re-entered in
a new square made arena, out of breath
and feathered in mucous slime, alive and raucous,
risking the rock garden show of all my own.

I'm only the spectator, folding up
and putting by, not sitting on, his raincoat,
but selecting rock, who taking off his glasses
reads the bill. *But this must be my bill for being
nearly healed.* It's headed *Believe it or not.*

An audience of smiles and whistles
calms my ripples. I feel so well-heeled, and swelling,
I'd be flopping like a cloth on water too,
it's just a list:
                    The Great Dame
                    Iris Pseudacorus.
        The bituminous forest and a feast of yeast
            as that which passeth into coma.
                    The Aroma
                of a Spiritual Beast.
            The prickle nettle-rash.
        A fainting in a windy passage.
        Supernatural, the crew of all the usuals
        who start to squeal and steal the show.

A worm in the beak of a bird regarded me
abnormally absurdly as it smiled
before it turned into a dark mill-doorway.
All the following was swilled into the mild.
I fell mistaken on the sill. *An Elf?
The Very Devil? Flying Snake? What Flew?*

It slides in loosely landing on the lake, as swish
as a swashbuckling Drake, or else the Striding Shadow
of a Puck upon a Stick. You have to answer!
        Duck?

Come out, come down, from over out beyond
The Seldom Seen, The Angry Brow,
The Riddle of The Southport Nile. What's there?
I couldn't make a square however hard I tried.
        The sea is like a rumour on the vision's edge.
The waste is marinated flat.
The channels may seem uterine, and not
the worse for that, but I could make no sense of being
fallen in the formless muck, afloat and flooding
with a rise of tide.
        A thoughtless guess is that I might be being
victimised by high reactions of the state.
        The history. The hissing is for *Mother Goose*,
A Masque of The Eternal Flame.
        The blame I took between the wings,
heartbeat in fear of language. Feathers,
Father: Do we suffocate the thing?

Brash ripple. Brittle rash erupts, a range from outrage
out to out and out applause,
up on the cusp of an ecstatic scream:
        May I burn
        in the rising font of my rebirth
        and be discovered
        in the person of a dove.

I tingle in the silence when I'm glad I came.
It didn't hurt much, did it? It had been far worse
if you had not been born, you'd not be
feeling better. Yes I guess I'd better
thank the regulars. It's good to be free, single,
light, light blue, light green, and somewhat
        satiated, soft and wetter.

Reed Raft across Mere Moss

How palpably my resignation as a creature
bleats in its distress! How troubled, falling,
clambering the intervallums, that so designated
failure struggles to confess its mess.

Its senses blend, beat, bend. A tree drawn
bleeds toward the storm. The thing's eye shrinks
    into a leaden sea.

A run like scree. The face collapsed.
A look of sheer credulity.
It can't have got across.
It must be drowned by now.

    A messenger came as a bird.
The swallow, having swum
    the foam and froth, through stifling hot
and muffled nothingness of air
has crossed the barrier.

These fumes and fences, Sir, it says,
do but assume offences. Of thy resignation
there is now no trace. I'd best be off
and on the job. But look thee there now
is that not the very spoil we seek
beneath thy feet, down in the mud?

Dull Nud, just as I thought,
    No Good.
The snake leafs into blood.

Slithering in slimes across the haggard grough
beneath a boiling smoke of swealing heather
slides our *Hairy Serpentine.* The Unresigned
re-slithers to deliver messages
        of Self Unkind.

Slipping on cold wet churchyard flags
the flummoxed thing slid through
a cold wet mulch of early leafmould,
spattered by a downspout gargoyle—

Call him *Pisser-in-the-Rough.*
The perishing and broken one
        has almost had enough.

He has been stuck with, for a servant
Rotten Rubber Muddy Lubber,
calling *Master!*
We are bound to seek
        a Throne across the Sky!

Washed up upon a coast of wild belongings—

Is this not Mad Wharf, beyond
the Wilderness of Formby? Nay,
        so forlornly there is us:
We are approaching Nowhere
and I don't know why.

It was a small and broken thing
that had inhabited a ruined hall
whose lawn ran wild.
    It spun a span, suspended spider
taking gleeful insects from the sun
into the rockslide glade.

And still they spiral
under leafage shade.

Emaciate Snakeface coiled upon the ladder
for a far escape.

The gawp looked like the ghost
within the home, its own unburied hole.

It looms as if accepting offered oral sex.
It routs among the leaves.
Let us relax.

When, squeaking sharp, it slipped
into the blue flat bloom below
subliminal, the sky slowly revealed
a yellow-brownish scumbled stew,
the dawn of sickness, vinegary discord,
        viscous glue, a rancid gloom.

Unclean silence fronds across the causeway
sprouting fungal blewits from the rotten wood.

A squirrel on the crest was rattling at
the wrought-iron gate.
        The point of healing ever disappearing
in the fountain square. But something, having
slipped ahead, was pumping up a draught.
A reed raft bumps the sluice
and passes through across the mort mere moss—
to the blue deeps of laughterless fate
        is my guess.

The Heron Rose toward a Cloud of Gold.
A warmth drawn high in dry expressive air.
And still the bright enigma hangs
        suspended there.

A Lancashire Chimæra

The ribbon dribbled, as a full-blown windsock
flopped. The water rippled, as the tidal Ribble
dropped. A thrilling treble flutes after the watch has
    stopped.

The spirit river filters through the stones—
    a dipper bobs about a bit
and flowing pools through boulders.

And what breathes upon the waters is itself a face.
No host so terrible,
    the spirit of white water race.

A bush of heather flowers
on a wide and ragged shoulder, wild
with pollen and aroma.

Lower flows and feeling colder,
though the colour rose to ruby,
there she glows.

The river runs out where a goat bleats
    at the rising sea.
I see Chimæra on the rim,
    and I shout She!

A catch sprung on the Jack.
A biff came from the box.
A bird rose where ventriloquy is baffled.

So a raucous thing came spoking through the throat
and talking
     Phoinos, Furness, Furnish, Fairness,
wrapping round the shoulders of a coat.

A bleating off the shielding on the cape.
The shadow of a flame that scarfs me
    like a snake.

Discarding glances in the wooden glade
it seeks the shade and stillness of
mere tarn or lake before the open channel
and the dreadful sound
in an unworthy boat.

Its hands about its ears
it cannot stand to hear
the awful deep uncoiling of a gong gone wrong;
the wrenching of a thumb;
the glottal choking of a song
so it must sit, quake, shimmer,
    wait.

Cheer up. The birds are bringing some
fresh garlanding, with bubbles
effervescent from a spring-flushed trough,
sufficient breath, fresh atmosphere
    and fair fresh air.

Across the awful mudflats came the awful train.
Throughout the storm I paddled at
      the limits of my brain,
A Flagrant Row. The Crying Babe.
A thing with wriggling fingers that
      is hardly born, and as yet lacks a name.

The clock of life despatching in discharge
departing sadness on the air
      as Triton blew it: fluid blueness
through the river's horn.

I saw a fighting couple on the night breeze wasting
sonant obloquy upon the air
      across a city square of trees.

A fluke of light, a beauty. The placenta of the earth
burst from the centre of the sphere of birth,
a spectral shower of snakes.
      The humming gate is drummed
to a diminished pinpoint, brightening in pitch.

The drab takes to its ditch at night.
An endless river flourishes at fringes.
Flickering of leaves across the road.
The shining from the banks of sand.
      On Hesketh Bank, on Warton Sands,
            the Estuarine Light!

Within the shell, shed, cellar
of the thing indwelling, downward
must be inward, to the ruins of foundation.
That way ran the hatched egg's diaspora
as forest snakes fan from the demon sphinx
and the horn is blown to glory
from the battlements and fine entitlements,
the pennants flutter, penance humbles,
peasants mutter an unpleasing mumble.

There I saw the thought of spirit froth
saw through the branching tree.
        Two doves fly free.

A dashed handful of marbles
on a tin tray tipped the scales
and then the silence, insects, water, yellow flags
and *Iris, Venus, Juno* through the silence rose.

Into this in-tray enter. *Duck*
beneath the Briar Rose. The birds are blown
as spirit globes.
        Saida, saith The Soul,
The Twins are Newly Born
        and chosen, shown.

Pretend the infinite may be refined;
the Shimmerer is kind;
the evolution and erosion of a love
cupidinous arose unblind.

With a friend and guest, curling down through
the wood, under overlooping branches
in beneath the blowing wind, I did propose
that love itself has suffered no substantial diminution,
but the appetite itself elects refinement—
    Casting darts of sight into wood deeps—
and appetite is drawn into the heart of what an
hesitance had quite mistaken for the silence.
There is no such thing,
    Bang Bang,
I snorted that I thought it had been appetite
that made it musical and
    Bang Bang, bang
an appetite's original was making noises long before
the lustful overture began.
    Bang.

But nothing suffers diminution.
Waters trickle in a showy swirl
and run upon a sudden.

Wind has suffered nothing
as it lifts and drops. The light
in leaf along the glade has lit
thy neck, thy crest, thine eyes,
thy rising and thy falling scales.

Our fingers intertwine. And so we slide,
glide, wind up down along
the greenwood footpath lanes. I trust
    love may be sane.

The Fountain Tree: The Paradisal Tuba

I.
Spirit of Rain in the Glade, sad day
plucked at with cutting glances plays
The Lamentation Serenade to Plant-Life
on the stops as plot synopsis:

Glowing with your own original and ringing
    golden sense of goodness and
of innocence, you sing out volunteering:
    I will take the Blame, even as far as
Absence, and with Luck come back
    like from an errand to the shops.

So tipped you dropped into the pit
like bucket-slops. Your glow is quickly lost.
    The little sibyls whisper,
flutteringly silver:
    Shall we bring The Listener
to The Songthrush now, or not?

Lips parting at the fountain crown emit
    a spirit-bubble, balancing on top, it pops
and spatters out in drops.
    And there's a fellow in a peaked cap
waving arms to bring the fabulous
    imaginary creature down.
It's like a goose, that fountain-tree of spirit,
playing fast and loose
    with the excuse of pure caprice.

II.
A falling globe burst, frittering
a rain of light upon the swollen
river-torrent, hurrying in through into
the infinite black inward sea, that's permanent
you think, and nothing personal
to me nor you, where one bright song breaks
bitterly on the subjective ear before it takes
the dark blue tunnel to that antique well
      of ink.

The blamed thing shrinks
into a pinhole silence whence
a blaring flume of chimney smoke
blooms out across the queasy lake.

There's reddening in evening rain.
A warm wind flushes, flourishes and washes clean
the ruby flutes, the sandy flats, a scale of notes.

A clown comes stumbling from the wings
armed with a brush and limewash bucket,
mumbling on about
    Abaddon who secures our loss
forever in the Nothing that is never done;
    Apollyon, The Devouring One,
the clown sings as he sinks his boat
or swims within the hearing of that fearful river.

III.
A genius of the sheer herbaceous sheen
stands greening like a stone, churning
the flow into a turbulence described by
strings of baling-twine and billowing tarpaulin,
uncontrollable, until the wind subsides,
and it's as if the uprising had never been.

The train attenuates, the shape has flown
and it's a warm night underneath the moon.
The spirit tunes upon an even channel
and displays the shown, a drain on screen
to draw the slough off slack and clough by draught
of rushing slaps along the open channel
        out to ocean, ridden on the tide
and there to float

        a snake, a flame, a flute,
            a goose, a goat,

it pipes its cumuloidal larkstwirls,
violet plumes and squirrel tails
on either side of parturition, equably
in numbers, shedding leaves of red
as suddenly as blood out by the throat
the thought-shape images its outer utterance.

IV.
Its leaves are like sigils for tears,
the sallow, whence a featherbreasted
songster squanders scribble, speckled like
a shower of bubbles bursting upon sense
with what seems like the joyousness of
    nonsense.

Hear them bubbles come obscured,
disordered, as through fronds
of bladderwrack and carragheen.

You thought you heard a *Tuba*, one of many
pompous brasses, brayed, blown, bloated,
drowned by tympani against a tidal moan;
but ruby-toned, sad grace of soul, sour sorrel:
    You can only go to turmoil once
down one long alley-way
    in single file.

It burst into eternally lost happiness.
The grey dove wobbles down
upon a nest of cloud.
The sun has settled as an even rose.

The smile was like one thrill of lights
upon a pinpoint when
the bubble of the sun had burst
in like a rain and then the oscillation gone.

V.

Azazel bleats upon the shoal. The clouds unfold.
Nowhere to go but drop a sack below the raft
beyond the flats. The pit of stars ahead
is bottomless and dead. A puffed-up dove
with captain's cap plays guide and pilot,
feathers streaming from its bill:

> *Why, Gentlemen,*
> *we have been stranded on The Shores of Sheol,*
> *that is, Hell, where spirit flounders*
> > *gobble globs of phlegm.*

But what's the blessed mystery of them balloons?
A rising company with trailing strings raise bristles
from the ghouls of broom stuck at the level-crossing.
Night-Birds streaming from The South sweep up
with pleasant faces. Bats or moths. You're
someone lost. You watch the nothing
> trickle through subsiding grounds.
You cannot guide yourself across the tidal dazzle
> to the fabled nest.

An open mouth rose in the pool.
The guide resigns with,
> *I am lost.*
Abandoned punters muddle on.
The goods rush by us betters
thundering into the best crash bonfire
westward in the estuary mist.

VI.
A sacred jug fills nothing from within.
A reservoir up in the hills that never fills
fed by a spring that never fails —
but one felt nothing but with nothing in.

There were no duller basement than
    The Phœnix Underground,
where sound feels slower
than a pudding-clock wound down,
and no-one laughs at such a cloud or clown
who cries out loud:

Now Saddle me this Wish
    That I might Ride the Bridal Nymph
        This spellbound night tonight.

And then the dawn flash cracked conceptual,
a speckled hen who laid an egg
of purple blood and solar flowers yolked
in colder slithery and moony body slides.

It sheds a skin as livery
disseminating in an oscillation on dilemma,
silvering and minnowing in eggshell,
    showing a variety
before the birth come forth
    the seahorse snakes
dispersing severally radial.

VII.

What crank or spirit pump is churning up
them bubbles then? High spirits rise like vines
and end in tears, shed sunlight, spears
retreating down the water-tree in streams
and bedding in the soil. You see them then
uncoiling off a heap of unwashed cloth
and rising slithery across
      your blinded eyes. You prophecize:
            I cannot see....
but silver bended mugwort
and the sprite of yellow ragwort clamour
by the roadside.
      Spiralling in Spheres,
the scales fall from your eyes.

You see a figure dancing on the fire-escape,
and rings of minnowy or moony quickness
shimmer on reflection from the roofslates
echoing an endlessly diminishing dilemma on
imperfect cadence, broken by a flourish, finish,
fusion, pluming through a fist of tears.

The valley-room is flushed and swilled
with a capacious sense of sacrificial fitness.

Now the figure dances to a kiss in mid-
career.
      It's you it means.

VIII.
No riddance from the croak that grates
across a blamed bypass estate.

A bleeding weeping creature in the balsam waits
to exit on the crack of brightness. Then it breaks
the scales and sheds its shell, to take the shape
of natural self or spill
    as yolk across the plate.

You see it like a phonic flame, a risen floating solo
falling, seeming inexhaustible in coils
like from a hosepipe rainbow snake,
it swills the dirt.

As the rain sets a term to the drought, it's explained
of the radiance there is nought to count,
but the drains, as the overflow fills,
and the plumes it spills, and the light
you have caught's moving out.

Listening, you hear the distant swash,
a lapping in the universal softness
    like a flight of moths
around the landing of a water-bird whose leafs
    are shed in fires of light like bright scintillas.

Now at evening when *The Tuba* droops
    into the blue nocturnal soup,
The Phœnix sinks within itself
    and sleeps.

Singleton's 10p Recital

1–5

This immense blue loneliness cannot originate
in me alone, can it? A quarry blast
    and rooks lift off tall trees.
While I was trying to tie a button on
a torn shirt sleeve, a warm March wind
was splashing at the door.

Comes my identical, a spirit baffled to be here.
The many doors I fear were less than welcoming
    to a toothless whistle.
Denizen insiders do their business
in their sentences, in squiggles of calligraphy,
inhabiting the stone-wall holes
they do in deed like rabbits.

Dippers run the sallowed pebbles.
Falls glissade to cold green holes.
Your single soul is shallow
    where the river swirls.

A living fistula of sinuosity was laid out by
the index finger on the plate in sunshine
    as a slime.

A Clown pretends to look into
    the dark sky heart along a cardboard tube:
The Stars My Eye! The cylinder squirts back reply.
    Have I been in The Wars!
The Siren Sings. We'd better turn to shelter now,
    for it comes on serious rain.

A bush erupts beside an empty house.
A woman in the thistle-field
feeds bread to mostly crows.

It was my hope the spiky moorland spirit fits
of spooks had decomposed, just when it leapt
the banking battily, ran the stream
and made its landing at my feet.
Indeed, it took me over, standing in my shoes.
It's lucky that I didn't have my glasses smashed
or get a bloody nose for such
belligerent behaviour as had ensued.

A sink had formed under the sandstone flags,
and floods the cellar floor. In that depression
there I saw the face of
                    Peggy Slitherer, the
Old Asphyxiate in form.

The cat has brought another squealing rodent
        to the door.
A sheet of falling swarms of worms
obscures and curtains water under ropes of rain
in storm. Flood overwhelms the draining
        of the moor.

There was a Siren shape, recall
        bent over in her shawl
to do ablutions at the only pool in miles.

As I sat gazing blankly at the black glass light
one night I saw a light-green fire-streak meteorite
slide down behind the pane. Remember when
the purple light had puzzled on the sandy marram
somewhere, and uncoiled across the dunes.

The brush-head broom brushed up the steps.
A pool through clefting trees had shone.

And then they dragged a drugged and drowsy
trooper down, and bagged his trousers.
His life for him had been from mouth to arse
one comic flap, a flat, a flame, a raft,
        a fart, a clap, a splat, a clasp,
a spit, a crack, a smack.

What frights thee? Has thou seen a *Corposant*?
Didst foil its furling coil
        to fork its branching tail?

I dropped the skin into a tin waste-paper bin.
The panes of glass were splattered with the rains
        of prickled occultry and wildernessy glazes.

Up on the upland now *Grimalkin* dost thou Graze
on Scapegoat Hill? And do they hold the *Asherah*
        with primal zeal there still?
Hast'ou come out in precathartic
        brightness now or what?
Thou brazen ass and shining calf,
Azazel has thine other half.
The simpleton'll leap to rhymes with *Kill*.

There was a RedCross Cock won great renown
    among the gulls of town.
Plumed like a great mill-chimney,
    he would drive them up and down.

I watched The Father give that gorgeous bird
the chop one Sunday Morning on the block.

Churchbells were sounding and The Boys' Brigade
were tuning up.
    The headless spectacle
ran spouting blood, amok.

A warm drain belched and spattered,
    rose and grey.

I ran to find my refuge out across the waste of weed
    and cinder.

Men still shovel ashes on the river-swirl.

All day there had been like a Pan. The horns
though had been more like antlers,
    girdled round with snakes.

The kids, but who's to worry, all go giddy
on The Walzer, throwing out free shrieks.

But one fine night they threw the brakes,
    cut engine, drew in sirens, and a dead one,
youngling,
    had been stretchered off.

Make room to stretch a change of guest.
    Priapus reappears refreshed,
knocking clappers on his knees and dressed
    in pantaloons and dancing clogs.

Make room for matey,
    dainty matelot,
(at whom the lads look daggers)
with a hornpipe tucked in spats.
    His back is arched
and jutted like a cat's
    ringed in with bandogs.

Make room at last,

(but the Clown was a great disappointment,
he looked lazy and inadequate,
and all he got was one
impertinent and bitter brittle laugh.

He called his simpleton's recital
Miracle Asylum. Funny it was not).

6–8

Fulgor lights the fall of
Troy, I think it must have been in flame.
Disaster spat, but licks soft curling hair,
and a great wash of phooey slid out there.

Out of subcutaneous crackling sprang
spontaneous fire. Then earth that standing maiden
naked with a nest of snakes.

Cleaning out the attic, I was crouched
under a ladder quaking in a dazzle
at a clatter from the cavern of the doves.
I doubled in the shadow on the landing stair.

For three days in the barking dark
I heard of harpies sporting obscene wombs
but couldn't speak for all the shit and ordure,
stricken dumb by pubic hair.
　　They wore no shorts, but only shirts
and every hair was in and out of
an alive performance in profound disorder,
　　an unkempt nightmare.

On the rush and backwash,
at the back of the throat,
Lamentation, guided, takes its place
at the back of the boat,
on the scrafe, in the pebbles' undertow,
　　Holy Surf!
Alive, alight, it doesn't burn.

The crystal sky spread out above the caravan
incredibly beautiful! The chrysolite
showed chloral light. The whole was domed
with bright cave coping, in a field
of lapis lazuli, and all beyond description.
Never in a month of sundays could I tell the value
any more than fill eternity with tales of
orbs in burble, papal ones, monarchicals—
We'd seen the lot, and felt belittled.
We could neither keep nor hold our marbles
in so capital a company and plot as this
without it grasps the throat and chokes a bit
        in bitter jest.

At bottom trough agreed to have been done with
dome disaster, dome disorder, so much water
in the storm, but hold the heart, its
inextinguishable palpitations in the palm.

Look once upon the twisting sea so calm.
Out over Lancaster, my heart has gone heraldic, —
Lancaster, Lancaster! Where are thy Caravans for Rome?
or Cartmel, Pilling, Preesall? All deflating,
        hardly harmed, but coming home.

First one, but many of my countrymen
are coming after, often dafter than I am,
beneath a wild sky, over sand.
Come tumbling cloud convovulations! I could have you
tabulated, tickled, tailored and reticulated
for the spirits of the heart to land in on demand.

Floats on a black wind.
Breakers race.
The shoal a flowing girdle.

My heart broke within me
when I passed by thy dwelling
boarded up.

A broken pier. Scrap metal by the ton.

A cupboard opens and
an oystercatcher flock lifts off.

The crashing in of banks to flood.
The what we did.
The river bed of weeds and mud.
The hollow cove of grass.
The green and grey.
The silver dale.
Another mudbank crashes.

Flock bleeps out on mussel bed.
The what we said.
A ton of feathers on my head.
A ton of lead.

A single seagull and a simple tune.
The fall of Troytown
on the Banks of Lune
whence all the indigenes are flown.

9–10

Give me a tone, a tune, a single tune.
We lost a lot of books at Waterloo.
A box of tricks was mislaid too.
     And I had come a cropper on her cheap
tin whistle. One bright night we two
were caught up in a right *feng-shui*
     sort of show.

As I drove over Axe Edge Moor
I parked myself the car and heard them laughing
from the water sports.
I keep my coat some distance from
the party in the showers. Surely
this is not my home. Then it starts,
not a hurt but in to rain.

Would it be sad to say that he had
stuck to rubbers while she bled?
     We know the steps they took
go only deeper down and out to dole.
     Or is it mad to lie and read
your griefs in bed, cap on a peg, protected only by
a thumbsneck latch on matchboard door?
     Three shy fair heads down there.
The shells and gourds may rattle,
hatching prattle, the full emptiness
     of our genetic egg.
The senseless horn the handsome snail,
     its calcium shell swirl.

But then the sky cleared and the outline fell shone
silvered with a branch of living water.

Could this be me? I'd have to see myself
        Hysterically Laocoön,
in twisting coils convulsed, but with
the snail, for horns and trace for trail.
        But I'll be always saving half or more
for Kitty at The Core. Sealed in,
I cannot hear so crazy jar.
You realise it is my conscience
        railing at the bar.

How deeply penetrated she had been essayed
whose barking cries on lips dried unresolved,
unthroated, swallowed down. The very dogs of love
at such, so protean a loveliness, at stop held off.
The flirting crow. Come hither trump, befriend.
Take my two wingbeats and a wide umbrella. A
saliva salivation. Leave thy mug out on the stump.
I'll play a right philaster in a balaclava
        and a dressing-gown with looking-glass.
And there the bark discharged its fraught.
A sable demon chalked one for the lads up
on a crested front. Best sensibility had felt betrayed.

Or else canst please me, ease this petulant
who pleads poor petals and whose nose is blown
        on leaves; whose idle lakes
leave puzzles in a naked heart's bestartlement;
but plumps the pith from throat to throne
        of that which having flown ye seek
and may not find, although it fly
        above the gate a tone too high:
If I were you we had let go the whole balloon.

Printed in the United Kingdom
by Lightning Source UK Ltd.
120167UK00001B/163-198